DEVELOPMENT CENTRE STUDIES

THIRD WORLD DEBT AND FINANCIAL INNOVATION

THE EXPERIENCES OF CHILE AND MEXICO

BY
HOSSEIN ASKARI

DEVELOPMENT CENTRE
OF THE ORGANISATION FOR ECONOMIC CO-OPERATION AND DEVELOPMENT

Pursuant to Article 1 of the Convention signed in Paris on 14th December 1960, and which came into force on 30th September 1961, the Organisation for Economic Co-operation and Development (OECD) shall promote policies designed:

- to achieve the highest sustainable economic growth and employment and a rising standard of living in Member countries, while maintaining financial stability, and thus to contribute to the development of the world economy;
- to contribute to sound economic expansion in Member as well as non-member countries in the process of economic development; and
- to contribute to the expansion of world trade on a multilateral, non-discriminatory basis in accordance with international obligations.

The original Member countries of the OECD are Austria, Belgium, Canada, Denmark, France, Germany, Greece, Iceland, Ireland, Italy, Luxembourg, the Netherlands, Norway, Portugal, Spain, Sweden, Switzerland, Turkey, the United Kingdom and the United States. The following countries became Members subsequently through accession at the dates indicated hereafter: Japan (28th April 1964), Finland (28th January 1969), Australia (7th June 1971) and New Zealand (29th May 1973). The Commission of the European Communities takes part in the work of the OECD (Article 13 of the OECD Convention). Yugoslavia takes part in some of the work of the OECD (agreement of 28th October 1961).

The Development Centre of the Organisation for Economic Co-operation and Development was established by decision of the OECD Council on 23rd October 1962.

The purpose of the Centre is to bring together the knowledge and experience available in Member countries of both economic development and the formulation and execution of general economic policies; to adapt such knowledge and experience to the actual needs of countries or regions in the process of development and to put the results at the disposal of the countries by appropriate means.

The Centre has a special and autonomous position within the OECD which enables it to enjoy scientific independence in the execution of its task. Nevertheless, the Centre can draw upon the experience and knowledge available in the OECD in the development field.

Publié en français sous le titre :

INNOVATION FINANCIÈRE
ET DETTE DU TIERS MONDE :
LE CAS DU CHILI ET DU MEXIQUE

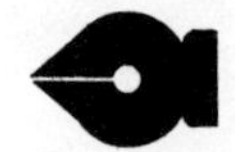

*

* *

This study was undertaken as a part of the Development Centre's programme on the theme of Financing of Development. It was carried out by Professor Hossein G. Askari in his capacity as a Consultant to the Centre.

TABLE OF CONTENTS

Chapter 3

Debt Management in Mexico

Chapter 4

Sufficient Debt Relief

Future Prospects

ACKNOWLEDGEMENTS

I have benefited from many sources in the preparation of this study. Many colleagues at the OECD Development Centre have made invaluable contributions: Dimitri Germidis guided me, Alexandra Papalexopoulou and Axel van Trotsenburg contributed numerous ideas. Bankers and officials involved in the debt situation clarified my thinking on numerous points. George Washington University, where I teach, has supported my endeavours over the years.

Mahmoud Wahab and especially Scheherazade S. Rehman assisted me in the preparation of this work. Stella Moody was a patient typist. To all of them, I express my sincere gratitude.

PREFACE

Debt in itself represents a formidable problem, both for borrowing countries unable to meet their repayment obligations and lenders unable to recoup their losses, but it has further implications for future growth, external finance and investment. This long-term effect will endanger development long after the immediate problem of repayment has been overcome.

Professor Hossein Askari of George Washington University, whose work in the field is well known, looks in detail at some of the financial innovations used to counter the problem of debt overhang and to overcome the threat of financial shortages in developing countries. Among other proposed solutions, he examines the much-criticised "Brady Plan" and finds that it may not be so inappropriate as some would have us believe. The current debate about debt reduction rarely strays into the realm of debt overhang, taking the short-term view and telling less than the whole story. Professor Askari takes a different approach and here attempts to correct this imbalance, using two case studies: Chile and Mexico.

This approach is particularly useful since the two countries are not only on the same continent – Latin America – but both shared a similar increase in their external debt in the critical 1979-1982 period, when the world wide crisis became apparent. Since then, however, their performances have been very different. Askari concludes that the difference was in the macro-economic policies followed by each country, and that on this basis the Brady Plan could have had more success in Chile than in Mexico.

The study concludes with an enlightening analysis of future approaches to the debt problem in general and calls for a re-assessment of attitudes by both lenders and borrowers.

Readers will find this a very useful handbook for understanding the complexity of the debt problem and it will stimulate further reflection on the search for solutions to the yawning problem of debt overhang.

Louis Emmerij
President, OECD Development Centre
April 1991

EXECUTIVE SUMMARY

Overview

At first the debt crisis was seen as a short-term liquidity problem. More recently it has been seen as a global predicament, affecting not just heavily indebted nations but the international economic system. Although the menu approach may have somewhat ameliorated debt servicing problems, economic performance in Third World countries remains unsatisfactory. For many of the distressed commercial debtor countries, sustained economic recovery in industrial countries, reduced real interest rates and protectionism, and most importantly appropriate domestic economic policies, are required to restore economic growth and improve creditworthiness. Many plans have been proposed to develop and maintain these desirable conditions. These plans have received little support from creditor institutions and governments. Most projects only envisage debt relief in the context of a zero sum game, not only lacking creditor support but possibly detrimental to debtors in the long run, cutting off their access to commercial credit. Other plans involve a turn-around in debtor policies but still receive little encouragement from either creditors or debtors.

Some new directions exist. Since creditors are now potentially willing to absorb discounts on Third World debt, it is possible to construct a less painful solution. A new approach would have to be far-reaching and realistic, but above all it must secure the commitment of creditor and debtor governments and creditor institutions. Debtors must incorporate reforms and policies that restore creditor confidence. Without this confidence, the problems could become insurmountable. As commercially indebted Third World countries lose market access, their inadequate growth will have negative implications for the global economy. The essence of the Brady Plan – debt reduction – tries to prevent this, though perhaps within a vacuum of too little assessment of the debt situation from the perspective of both creditors and debtors.

Chile's and Mexico's External Debt

Chile's and Mexico's external debt, like that of other major debtors, has greatly increased since 1975. During the period 1979-1982, it was not accompanied by a permanent increase in fixed investment and growth. The more recent decline in debt service payments has been due to falling interest rates and refinancing, resulting in lower amortization payments. Innovative debt management policies in Chile have also ameliorated the debt service burden.

Debt Management in Chile

Chile's external debt belonged mainly to the private sector in 1982. The situation was reversed in 1988: public sector debt became the major component. Government guarantees of substantial private sector debt, demanded by creditor banks and readily agreed to, has been an important factor in transforming the debt picture.

Chile has been successful in reducing interest rate spreads on its debt and extending maturities through renegotiations. In the other area of debt reduction (repurchases and conversions), Chile lowered its external commercial debt by $4.2 billion (from December 1984 to June 1988). The lion's share of reductions, about $3.2 billion, have been in the private sector.

Chile's success stems from beneficial macro-policies, especially the containment of domestic budgetary deficits and the consolidation of gains from economic restructuring. In addition, Chile's repurchase and conversion schemes have been well conceived and stable.

Debt reduction in the future may be more difficult for two reasons. First, much of the external debt is now concentrated in the public sector, making repurchases and particularly conversions more difficult. Second, private sector debt has declined while private sector foreign exchange for these repurchases is more limited and assets for converting may be less available. Nevertheless, Chile appears to have its external debt more under control than do other major Latin American debtor-countries.

Debt Management in Mexico

Although Mexico's external debt increased radically in the years before 1982, it was largely made up of capital flight. Since 1982, the creditor composition of Mexico's external debt has changed considerably. In 1982, commercial creditors represented about 82 per cent of outstanding credit to Mexico, then declined to less than 80 per cent of a larger volume of debt by late 1988. The change was a result of the end of voluntary lending to Mexico, with official creditors taking up the slack.

Reschedulings have improved the terms of Mexico's debt profile over time but the contribution of debt reduction schemes – debt-equity swaps and debt securitisation – has been smaller than expected. Mexico's debt-equity swap programme was not well planned and it induced higher inflation. The debt securitisation programme did not offer creditors enough incentives to participate. Both programmes did little to alleviate Mexico's debt service burden.

Besides general approaches to debt reduction, the outlook for debt repurchases and conversions by the public sector will depend on Mexico's future export performance (especially oil prices), on the government's budgetary situation, and on the design and continuity of Mexico's conversion programme. With respect to the budget, Mexico has developed severe problems and the outlook remains dim. The medium-term outlook on oil prices is not optimistic, given the existing excess production capacity in OPEC countries. Mexico can, however, change its conversion programme in several helpful ways, e.g.:

i) formally include Mexican nationals in the conversion and repurchase scheme, as in Chile.
ii) make use of auctions to capture more of the discount.
iii) use borrowing, as opposed to printing money, to finance conversions; the best policy will control government finances and reduce inflation.

iv) achieve continuity in its programme.

The Brady Plan may also make a strong contribution to resolving Mexico's debt problem.

Sufficient Debt Relief

Debt-related difficulties may have adversely affected investment and growth in heavily indebted countries. This effect, commonly referred to as "debt overhang", acts like a tax on current and future income and causes a large proportion of income growth to accrue to foreigners. "Sufficient" reduction in debt servicing during periods of financial difficulty would maintain investment, break the vicious debt trap and encourage higher investment and growth.

Calculations can only be approximate concerning the level of debt-service reductions necessary to induce acceptable growth. Even with good levels of reduction, one must still hope for better debtor policies. Debt reduction by itself cannot induce economic growth or enhance future debt-servicing capacity.

Conclusion and Future Prospects

Any approach to the debt problem would be assisted by the following measures:

i) more favourable accounting and tax treatment of debt transactions (sale, swap, loan-loss provisioning) for commercial banks and an eventual standardisation across countries;

ii) agreement by government creditors not to have their Third World credits treated as senior to commercial credits, and to make commensurate concessions on their Third World loans as commercial creditors;

iii) realistic proposals to tie debt-servicing to capacity, enhancing debtors' incentives for economic restructuring;

iv) economic co-operation in creditor countries to improve performance in their own countries and market access for Third World exports, and to adopt a unified approach to the debt problem;

v) better management of economic and financial policies in debtor countries to increase economic growth, productivity and debt-servicing ability, and consequently reverse capital flight.

The core of the author's argument for a more general solution than the menu approach to Third World debt is clear. With enough commitment and realism, the problem could be ameliorated to restore the confidence of commercial creditors towards much of the Third World, afford renewed access to credit, stimulate growth in the Third World and strengthen the long-term financial position of creditors. The more quickly confidence and growth are renewed in the Third World, the more likely it is that long-term commercial access will be restored.

The application of the Brady Plan in the case of Mexico raises the following questions:

i) the reduction of commercial debt should be attained through a negotiated discount that leaves banks engaged. This negotiation should induce *all* banks to participate. Unfortunately, in the rush to obtain an agreement for Mexico, it appears that some banks may balk. This could result in non-participating banks attempting to seize Mexican assets since the new securities will be, *de facto,* senior to loans. Under these circumstances it is unlikely that banks will remain committed to Mexican lending;

ii) it is uncertain, even if all banks participate, that the size of the debt-servicing reduction is sufficient to restore growth and enable Mexico to service its newly restructured debt;

iii) a useful feature in the plan would have been favourable revisions in tax and accounting treatment – these could have been offered as a "carrot" to induce all banks to participate;

iv) another advantage would have been more comprehensive conditions for servicing newly structured debt. This could have restored value to the Third World debt portfolio and created stronger policies in debtor countries;

v) finally, it is questionable whether the resources set aside under the Brady Plan can tackle Mexico's debt swaps, especially if all creditor banks opt for newly issued securities instead of contributing new money.

The political stampede to help Mexico may have precluded a more comprehensive approach. Mexico, which is not a likely success story under the Brady Plan, could provide an unsatisfactory example for other heavily indebted countries. The comparison of policies and developments in Chile and Mexico indicates that the application of the Brady Plan to Chile would be much more likely to succeed, and would give a signal to other debtors of the rewards of good policy. In any case, the new direction for resolving the debt trap is clear: debt reduction, which must benefit both debtors and creditors to achieve long-term success. Meanwhile the Brady Plan would be assisted by a de-politicisation of the debt situation.

Chapter 1

OVERVIEW

Introduction

During much of the 1980s, the Third World debt situation was referred to as the Third World debt crisis, with the word "crisis" conveying a different message at different times.

Mexico's debt-servicing difficulties were referred to in 1982 as the Mexican debt crisis. It was seen as a Mexican problem, with no imminent danger for other countries or for the international financial system. High interest rates reflected the demand for borrowing to service existing debt. Eventually the reduction in commercial lending that followed Mexico's debt-servicing problems, coupled with high interest rates and unfavourable terms of trade, transformed the problem into a crisis for several countries. As more and more Third World economies struggled to service debts, awareness grew of the potential detrimental impact on the international financial system. After bank regulators shored up the global financial system – mandating higher capital asset ratios and taking a more liberal attitude towards non-performing loans and tax treatment – attention shifted to the economic and financial difficulties, sometimes referred to as "debt overhang", of the heavily indebted countries, specifically the absence of acceptable economic growth (recent or projected)[1].

Debt overhang may have adversely affected investment and growth in these countries[2]. The grounds for such a presumption are that *(a)* the observed reduction in current account deficits to service external debt was made possible through a drop in domestic investment; *(b)* as the debt burden becomes excessive, debt-servicing becomes implicitly linked to economic performance. Thus higher debt-service payments act as a tax on current and future income (a large share of any future benefits accruing to creditors), reduce the return to investment and hence adversely affect investment levels. Countries faced with a debt-overhang do not have the incentive to undertake appropriate adjustments[3]. Therefore a vicious circle is created, catching countries in a debt trap.

The crisis has yet another potential manifestation that has received less recognition. Up to the mid 1970s, Third World countries had little access to commercial credit (private lending). Access to commercial credit by largely middle-income Third World countries has developed only over the last fifteen years or so. If the debt situation does not improve for creditors and debtors alike, access to commercial credit may soon be lost for most Third World countries, with ominous prospects for their long-term growth.

Since 1982, however, progress has been slow. The parties involved have mainly attempted to tackle the most immediate problems, and the governments of industrial countries have not worked in a co-ordinated, committed, long-term manner. International institutions do not have the resources or the mandate to solve the problem. Commercial creditors facing deteriorating balance sheets, especially in the United States, have been forced by de-regulation and increased competition into other business activities to improve their finances. Many debtor countries, with little room to manœvre, have adopted short-term goals, sacrificing investment and long-term growth. The exception is a handful of Asian countries which have used external borrowing to finance a diversified export base and achieve sustained growth.

The impact of the crisis has been demonstrated in the poor economic performance of heavily indebted countries (low economic growth, declining *per capita* incomes and discouraging economic conditions) and has in turn affected world economic output, reducing global economic activity and performance.

In the face of these problems calling for far-reaching cures, only temporary remedies have been adopted. The world has "muddled on", but not "muddled through" the debt problem.

The objective of this study is to put the Third World debt situation in perspective, to analyse the experiences of Chile and Mexico, and to survey possible solutions involving some debt relief for countries facing chiefly commercial debt. Much poorer countries, which are usually saddled with official debt rather than commercial, require debt forgiveness rather than debt relief.

Over-indebtedness of Developing Countries: the Present Situation

The growth of external debt of developing countries has been rapid (see Table 1.1)[4]. The fifteen heavily indebted countries[5], as their classification indicates, have borrowed deeply from commercial sources (derived from total debt minus official debt in Table 1.1); while the poorer developing countries have had to rely on official credits. Of the $1 194.8 billion in debt at the end of 1987, $745.8 billion came from commercial sources, nearly half of which had been extended to the fifteen heavily indebted countries ($352.1 billion). In Table 1.2, the debt-to-export and debt-service ratios are given for various groups of developing countries. Although recently there has been some marginal improvement in the ratios for the aggregate of all developing countries, the overall deterioration since 1976 is striking. The worst ratios are in the Western Hemisphere, which is weighed down by its large share of the fifteen problem debtor countries. Any aggregate picture still hides, unfortunately, the severe difficulties of certain individual developing countries, especially those with rescheduling problems.

The debt crisis that began in 1982 is actually composed of different types of crises for different country groups. The publicised crisis belongs to the heavily indebted (commercial debt) countries, as symbolised by the fifteen countries of the Baker Plan[6]. The other, no less real, is that of poorer countries in debt mostly to official creditors. For them, there is even less hope of gaining commercial credit, with their lower income levels and economic potential. Our study focuses on the commercially indebted developing countries, which with long-term co-operation between creditors and debtors and better domestic economic policies may still resolve their debt problem, enhance their creditworthiness, and re-acquire access to commercial credit[7].

For many of today's debtors, commercial credit was abundant in the 1970s when banks needed to recycle their petro-dollars and many Third World countries (more than it would seem prudent) were perceived as good credit risks. However, given their emerging debt-servicing problems, the flow of commercial credit abruptly halted in 1982, resulting in the

Table 1.1. EXTERNAL DEBT, BY CLASS OF CREDITORS, 1976-87

End year, in billions of US$

	1976	1977	1978	1979	1980	1981	1982	1983	1984	1985	1986	1987
Developing Countries												
Total Debt	276.1	343.5	424.8	534.3	635.8	747.7	846.6	897.0	942.0	1 016.6	1 099.0	1 194.8
Official Debt	95.6	114.7	138.1	168.0	191.3	215.6	244.8	271.6	296.5	340.3	392.4	449.0
Commercial Debt	180.5	228.8	286.7	366.3	444.5	532.1	601.8	625.4	645.5	676.3	706.6	745.8
15 Heavily Indebted												
Total Debt	112.4	138.0	179.1	219.9	271.0	332.3	379.7	393.6	406.5	420.4	442.0	466.4
Official Debt	21.3	25.4	30.5	33.2	37.6	43.2	48.6	59.4	67.5	80.0	97.6	114.3
Commercial Debt	91.1	112.6	148.6	186.7	233.4	289.1	331.1	334.2	339.0	340.4	344.4	352.1
Low Income, except India and PR China												
Total Debt	25.1	29.7	35.7	41.1	48.2	54.4	60.7	64.9	69.6	79.1	89.8	103.1
Official Debt	20.0	23.2	27.3	32.0	37.4	42.8	48.5	52.3	56.7	64.8	74.7	86.8
Commercial Debt	5.1	6.5	8.4	9.1	10.8	11.6	12.2	12.6	12.9	14.3	15.1	16.3

Source: IMF. For definition of country groups, see *World Economic Outlook*, IMF, April 1988.

Table 1.2. INDEBTED DEVELOPING COUNTRIES:
DEBT-SERVICE PAYMENTS ON SHORT-TERM AND LONG-TERM DEBT
1976-87

	1976	1977	1978	1979	1980	1981	1982	1983	1984	1985	1986	1987
Debt/export ratio												
Cap-Importing Dev. countries	113.8	120.3	126.3	123.1	114.0	128.9	155.3	164.1	156.9	172.5	184.3	171.9
With D.S. problems	137.5	147.1	163.2	165.0	152.0	186.5	240.3	253.8	244.1	265.4	304.6	298.7
Without D.S problems	91.1	95.0	93.4	85.8	79.4	81.4	92.9	100.1	96.2	110.5	115.1	106.3
15 heavily indebted	163.7	172.2	204.3	183.7	168.2	202.4	267.6	289.1	269.1	286.8	344.2	328.9
Low income except India & PR China	211.0	211.4	232.3	225.9	223.2	268.9	324.8	339.3	346.4	405.3	423.8	453.1
Sub-Saharan Afr. (except Nigeria & South Africa)	113.1	123.5	146.2	149.0	147.9	184.4	218.5	231.5	227.7	271.7	296.9	325.1
Debt-servicing/export ratio												
Non-oil Dev. countries	16.1	16.9	18.4	20.7	19.3	22.1	25.0	21.8	22.0	22.5	22.8	19.6
With D.S. problems	21.2	22.2	25.5	29.5	26.6	32.0	38.8	32.2	33.5	33.5	35.0	29.0
Without D.S. problems	9.3	10.2	11.6	11.6	11.2	12.7	14.5	14.8	15.4	17.1	18.1	16.7
15 Heavily Indebted	26.6	27.8	33.7	34.7	29.4	38.8	48.9	39.3	39.5	39.2	43.2	35.9
Low Income except India & PR China	16.9	15.4	14.3	13.6	16.3	19.8	21.9	23.7	26.1	28.6	28.4	27.5
Sub-Saharan Afr. (except Nigeria & South Africa)	12.2	12.1	14.0	15.1	16.8	20.2	23.1	22.7	25.5	26.9	28.5	24.5

Source: IMF.

failure of many developing countries to meet their debt-service obligations (previously fulfilled through additional borrowing). After the Mexican crisis of 1982, commercial credit to developing countries declined. This in turn resulted in slow growth, and in some cases the level of *per capita* income in 1987 dropped below that of 1980[8]. In 1988, the situation for Latin American countries was summarised by the managing director of the IMF:

> "From this analysis, though, a difference in perception has emerged. What is seen, and felt, in Latin America is that *per capita* real GDP is still 6 per cent lower than in 1980; that the volume of imports and the ratio of investment to GDP are each down by as much as one quarter; and that in spite of the adjustment achieved, external financing remains inadequate.
>
> Understandably, there is political weariness. What is seen by creditors, meanwhile, is that the ratio of debt to exports, although falling a little in 1987, is almost double its level in 1980; that inflation remains an acute problem, with large fiscal deficits swallowing a high proportion of domestic savings; and that in some countries conditions conducive to capital flight persist. This explains why there is reluctance to add to exposure"[9].

Development of the Debt Crisis

There are numerous explanations in the literature for the debt crisis. They fall into two categories – those basically outside the control of debtor countries (exogenous factors) and those largely of the countries' own making (domestic policy shortfalls)[10]. The problems of each debtor country are different and generalisations must be interpreted with caution[11].

The exogenous developments have been deteriorating terms of trade, slow growth and rising protectionism in industrial countries, and high interest rates on external debt.

The terms of trade of developing countries had been improving by about 6 per cent per year before 1978, but a marked reversal after 1978 led to its negative growth[12]. The increase in oil prices in 1979/1980, while helping some debtor countries like Mexico and Venezuela, hurt most debtors. Additionally, during the period 1978-1980, the IMF estimated the price change component of non-oil imports of all non-oil developing countries at around $50 billion – a figure widely in excess of the impact of oil price increases on these countries[13]. In 1981 commodity prices in real terms were at their lowest level since 1950 and some 20 per cent below those of the 1974/1975 recession.

The 1981/1982 economic recession in the major OECD countries, besides damaging the terms of trade of many developing countries, reduced demand for their exports[14]. Imports from developing countries were further curtailed because of heightened protectionist measures[15]. A symptom of this state of world economic affairs is seen in the annual growth percentage in the value of the non-oil developing countries' exports. This measure of their ability to earn foreign exchange showed a significant slowdown between 1980 and 1981 (6.3 per cent) and an even worse deterioration between 1981 and 1982, when the value of their exports increased by only 0.8 per cent over the year before[16]. These developments made it difficult for many non-oil developing countries to earn enough foreign exchange to satisfy their external obligations. The adverse impact on exports of developing countries was not, however, uniform. Some developing countries that had diversified their economies into manufacturing experienced rapid export expansion.

Another adverse exogenous development, affecting eleven developing countries, was rising euromarket interest rates. Monetary restraints that were imposed to reduce inflationary pressures, and the increasing budget deficits of OECD countries, resulted in a doubling of interest rates between 1978 and 1981[17]. It is estimated that the net proportion of floating rate debt for non-oil developing countries was around 45 per cent in 1982; for the deeply indebted countries this ratio was even higher[18]. Argentina had 70 per cent of its net debt tied to floating rates, Brazil 71 per cent, and Mexico 78 per cent.

Seventy per cent of net floating-rate debt of non-oil developing countries was owed by these three alone. Net debt increased at an average speed of 17.8 per cent a year, while net interest payments rose an average of 39.3 per cent a year (see Table 1.3). The wake left by these exogenous developments demonstrates part of the story behind the debt crisis – debt-servicing had become painful, difficult and prohibitively expensive by 1982, especially for the largest commercial debtors[19]. Right when these countries needed more financing to smooth out consumption, credit availability disappeared.

Shortfalls in debtor countries' economic policies also contributed to the crisis. A reflection of their inappropriate macro-economic methods (and of the external factors) was their cumulative current account deficit[20]. Between 1977 and 1981, the deficit of non-oil developing countries more than tripled, from $30.4 billion to $109.1 billion, after which it eased to $56.4 billion in 1983. These deficits, however were less and less financed by non-debt creating flows such as foreign direct investment or long-term loans from official creditors. While the share of non-debt creating flows used to finance current account deficits dropped from 33.6 per cent in 1977 to 23.8 per cent in 1981 and the share of long-term borrowing from official creditors dropped even more, from 31.3 per cent to 19.7 per cent, borrowing from private creditors increased from 43.8 per cent in 1977 to 64.1 per cent in 1980, only to decline from then on. Borrowing from commercial banks at shorter maturities and higher interest rates to finance current account deficits points towards structural problems and commercial banks' lack of attention to the purpose of these loans.

The unfortunate policies of debtor countries have included erroneous monetary, fiscal, exchange rate and commercial decisions and a variety of distortionary government regulations.

Table 1.3. EFFECT OF RISING INTEREST RATES IN THE EARLY 1980s ON NET INTEREST PAYMENT BY NON-OIL LDC'S RELATIVE TO THE RISE OF TOTAL NET DEBT

	1979	1980	1981	1982	1983
Increase in Net Debt	17	18	24	12	11
Increase in Net Interest Payments	39	46	33	39	–10

INTEREST COST AS A PERCENTAGE OF DISBURSED DEBT

	1979	1980	1981	1982	1983	1984	1985	1986	1987
Average Interest/Cost Floating Debt:	12.3	15.5	17.4	17.1	12.2	10.0	11.8	8.4	6.0

Source: *External Debt of Developing Countries,* 1983, OECD, *Financing and External Debt of Developing Countries,* 1987 Survey, Paris 1988.

Monetary policies have invariably called for rapid credit expansion, causing inflationary pressures, distortions and misallocation of resources. Large fiscal deficits, usually due to wasteful consumption subsidies and low return on public investment projects, have occurred at the expense of investment and long-term growth.

A macro-economic policy of aggressive fiscal expansion stimulated an appreciation of real exchange rates. This policy was sustained by continued external borrowing, producing a disincentive for the development and growth of the export sector. Because of the underperformance of exports, debt-servicing was made even more difficult.

Ill-conceived commercial policy and large and divergent tariff rates have contributed to an inefficient allocation of resources in favour of high-cost production for the domestic market at the expense of export industries. Government regulations curtailing foreign investment have resulted in reduced efficiency. Financial repression has engendered low and negative real interest rates, again misallocating resources and encouraging capital flight.

The general lessons from successful developing countries indicate that good performance requires government commitment to policies that increase the efficiency of resource allocation. The exact form of these policies may differ from country to country, but the core is the same – a stable course of macro-economic decisions, timely removal of controls, increased private sector participation, development of domestic capital markets and tax reform[21].

The 1982 crisis was first perceived as a short-term liquidity problem for some countries. Thus the initial response from 1982 to 1984 was a series of short-run measures and traditional case-by-case approaches applied to a new problem, or at least a much more pronounced form of an older problem. These approaches were:

- short-term debt rescheduling;
- securing additional financing for debtor nations;
- implementation of domestic policies for economic adjustment.

While rescheduling official debt has been conducted in an organised framework under the auspices of the Paris Club, and made conditional to an IMF programme, private debt rescheduling has faced obstacles. The sheer number of the parties involved in the negotiations has made reaching agreements over the terms a drawn-out, tedious task. Furthermore, the cost of extensions on principal and interest was quite high since banks generally charged a higher spread for the renegotiated loan as well as up-front fees at the time of renegotiation; banks asked for these terms to improve their short-term outlook and to demonstrate the increased risk associated with Third World lending. Ironically, these demands contributed to a more rapid deterioration of the debtors' financial conditions (and are therefore practised less today).

To prevent the economic collapse of some debtor nations, the flow of new funds had to continue. Initial emergency funds from the U.S. Federal Reserve Bank and the Bank for International Settlements for Mexico were meant to tide Mexico over until more long-term funds became available. The International Monetary Fund was instrumental in convincing banks to continue the flow of funds to the developing countries, by tying its contribution of financial resources for the domestic adjustment programme of borrowers to availability of new commercial financing.

The essence of IMF lending was to allow debtors to generate adequate foreign exchange resources to stay current on their debt obligations. The programme's objectives included:

- cutting the budget deficit to a manageable size so that it would not lead to a rise in inflation, an increase in domestic interest rates, or an accelerated need for foreign borrowing;
- some targets on domestic credit expansion to control inflation;
- some degree of exchange rate adjustment; and
- imposing a limit on the amount these nations could borrow consistent with their capacity to borrow (this ceiling did not cover soft loans).

These case-by-case efforts, though helpful, were not enough, and countries required frequent reschedulings[22]. These were reorganised through multi-year rescheduling agreements (MYRAs) from 1984 to 1986. These agreements recognised the long-range nature of the problem, but unfortunately, in many cases the adjustment policies that were part and parcel of MYRAs were not followed through.

Even countries that have had some success in improving their external position have experienced other difficulties[23]. For instance, Brazil has a large surplus on its trade account, but has been unable to service its debt. The booming private sector has invested its exports proceeds abroad, in part through capital flight, resulting in a massive current account surplus. The transfer of the surplus from the private to the public sector has been untenable because of other domestic economic problems. Under such conditions, countries neglect to promote private saving, growth and exports, focusing instead on collecting resources from the private sector to finance external debt. Consequently the underlying difficulty of problem debtor countries is the fiscal deficit of the entire public sector. Resources must be transferred from the private to the public sector before external transfers can be made. This internal transfer of resources is invariably hampered by fiscal rigidities and inflationary finance[24].

In 1986, some beneficial measures were added to reinforce rescheduling, financing and implementation of better adjustment policies in debtor countries. Thus, the "menu approach", conceived in 1987, was used in the 1988 package for Brazil.

The menu approach testified to the fact that it was difficult for creditor governments, international institutions, commercial banks and debtor countries to balance their interests and reach a common ground for quickly resolving the Third World debt problem. The approach evolved from the following sequence of events:

i) a co-ordinated solution, whether to improve world economic conditions (high growth in industrial countries, lower protectionism, lower interest rates and better debtor country policies) or to adopt a specific plan, was difficult at the international level;

ii) the initial approach – bridge financing, rescheduling, IMF/World Bank programmes – though useful, could not produce reasonable growth in debtor countries because of the long-term nature of the debt crisis;

iii) additional approaches (largely market-oriented), though individually only marginally helpful should have also been used; taken together they could result in sufficient growth, at least in some debtor countries.

The menu includes a host of options – new commercial lending, more lending by international institutions, rescheduling, new money bonds, exit bonds, trade credits, project loans, debt-equity swaps, and debt securitisation (like the Mexico-Morgan plan). Two of these, debt-equity swaps and the Mexico-Morgan plan (and possible variants), have received special attention. More recently, in 1989, the Brady Plan was proposed to include debt relief and debt forgiveness.

a) Debt-Equity Swaps (DES)

A straight debt-equity swap is the conversion of Third World debt into equity in a domestic firm or into other assets; as such it is an alternative to encouraging direct foreign investment or foreign portfolio investment[25]. Debt-equity swaps are also used to establish closed-end funds in Third World equities and to acquire exports. In some cases, the conversion does not involve a foreign purchaser but a local one, thus attracting both local capital from abroad and flight capital. In this study, debt-equity swaps will mean swaps from debt into equity proper, as opposed to other forms of conversions.

These swaps were formally introduced in Chile in 1985. Eight countries have had varying degrees of experience with them: Argentina, Brazil, Chile, Costa Rica, Ecuador, Mexico, the Philippines and Venezuela. At least nine others are now introducing, or are actively considering introducing, swap programmes: Colombia, the Dominican Republic, Egypt, Honduras, Jamaica, Morocco, Nigeria, Peru and Uruguay.

The attraction of debt-equity swaps to the investor, foreign or domestic, is that domestic currency is received at a discount from market rates (minus the transaction fee) for investment in the country. (For a brief overview of the features of these swaps in different countries see Table 1.4.)

Debt-equity swaps may result in major direct benefits for a country, in that they:

1. reduce the size of external obligations;
2. shift repayments to circumstances (i.e. domestic) over which the country has more control;
3. encourage investment that would otherwise not occur (additionality), enhancing debt-servicing ability if investments are in export-oriented industries;
4. improve the quality of existing investments by providing strategic stakes in projects or enterprises to investors with valuable expertise and technology; and
5. stimulate the repatriation of flight capital. The issue boils down to the impact of these swaps on the debtor's asset/liability structure: Will the partial reduction in debt-service payments be offset by an increased outflow of foreign exchange because of the foreign investor's repatriation of dividends and capital?

At the same time, debt-equity swaps have potential drawbacks. They may expand the domestic money supply, increasing inflation. If domestic bond markets are developed and savings are available, then the government may be able to finance the conversion through selling government bonds (sterilisation) instead. This, however, will increase domestic interest rates and thus the cost of financing domestic debt. Although external debt is reduced, the availability of new money from commercial sources may diminish. If the debt-equity programme is not well-planned, "round-tripping" of capital may occur – debt conversion followed by capital exports at a profit. Finally, these swaps are a form of subsidy for investments in particular sectors and therefore additional economic distortions may occur.

For the bank holding the debt, they offer an opportunity to receive at least some compensation for loans, while presenting difficult accounting decisions for the balance of the loans not converted. Also, because of the newly adopted international standard for capital adequacy, they enable banks to reduce relatively risky loans. For banks and non-

Table 1.4. FEATURES OF DEBT CONVERSION SCHEMES

	Argentina	Brazil	Chile[1]	Costa Rica	Ecuador[2]	Mexico	Philippines	Venezuela
Eligible Investors								
Non Residents								
Any Creditor	x		x	x	x	x[3]	x	x
Original Creditor only			x[4]					
Residents	x		x	x	x	x	x	
Eligible external debt								
Public Sector	x	x	x	x	x	x[5]	x[6]	x
Private Sector	x	x	x		x		x	
Exchange rate for conversion								
Official exchange rate	x	x	x	x			x	x
Parallel exchange rates	x[7]					x[7]		
Valuation of debt for conversion								
Face value		x			x		x[8]	
Below face value	x[9]		x[10]	x		x		x[11]
Eligible domestic investments								
Equity								
Parastatal enterprises			x			x	x	x
Private companies	x	x	x	x	x	x	x	x
Original obligor only	x[12]							
Debt								
Public Sector			x	x				
Private Sector			x		x			
Repayment of domestic obligations		x	x			x		
Restrictions on eligible investments								
Restrictions on capital repatriations	x	x[13]	x	x	x	x	x	x
Restrictions on profit remittances								
Same as for all foreign investment		x						
More restrictive than the above	x		x	x	x	x	x	x

Other features								
Limit on value of conversions	x		x	x				
Auctions of conversion right		x[14]						
Conversion fees						x	x	
Additional foreign exchange required			x	x		x[15]		x
Tax credits		x[16]						
Privatisation programme	x[17]	x[18]	x		x[18]	x[18]	x[19]	

1. Compendium of Rules on International Exchange, Chapters XIX and XVIII.
2. Introduced in February 1975 and temporarily suspended in August 1987.
3. Mexico has temporarily suspended receiving applications under the scheme in October 1987.
4. Before June 1984, any non resident could participate.
5. Rescheduled debt only.
6. Rescheduled debt and debt that falls due on or after January 1st, 1987.
7. Free market exchange rate.
8. Debt redeemed at face value, but conversion fees apply.
9. Discount, if any, determined by an auction.
10. Conversions of public sector debt are subject to a small discount; conversion terms of private sector debt are negotiable.
11. Discount, if any, determined by newly formed commission with oversight responsibility.
12. Private sector debt only.
13. Since March 1987, investment through debt conversion must remain at least 12 years in Brazil before becoming eligible for repatriation.
14. Chapter XVIII investments only.
15. Investments in the non-priority sector only.
16. Introduced in December 1982; eliminated in June 1984.
17. Active Privatisation Programme but debt equity not applicable.
18. Incipient.
19. Active sale of non-performing assets.

Source: The Economist, *Guide to Debt Equity Swaps,* London 1987. IMF, *International Capital Markets,* World Economic and Financial Surveys, January 1988.

bank intermediaries, debt-equity swaps have afforded large fees compared to other activities, sometimes up to 15 per cent of the market value, though normal fees have been around 5 per cent, and even these have declined.

The objective for the debtor country is reduced debt burden, enhanced creditworthiness, and thus increased flow of resources. The most important component of increased net flows is the current and future size of debt-equity swaps for individual Third World countries. On the supply side, this is limited by the debt that may become available either through the secondary market or through creditors directly converting for their own portfolios. The demand for these swaps depends on their attractiveness to investors: confidence in the economy and in the business climate, size of discount, investment opportunities in debtor countries, rate of return in debtor countries, and direct foreign investment policies of debtor countries, especially concerning repatriation of profits.

A second important question is how interest and principal payments under existing external debt structure compare with converted debt through debt-equity swaps. This requires a case-by-case comparison of expected discounted payments (interest and

Table 1.5. SECONDARY MARKET FOR DEVELOPING COUNTRY DEBT
1984-1988, US$ million

	Debt conversions[a]					All transactions	
	1984	1985	1986	1987	1988[b]	1987	1988
Highly Indebted Countries							
Argentina	31	469			1 507	750	2 260
Brazil	731	537	176	300	6 224	1 250	15 560
Bolivia					349		524
Chile		324	987	1 983	2 357	3 500	3 536
Colombia							0
Costa Rica			7	146			0
Ecuador				125	102		153
Jamaica				1	102		102
Mexico			416	6 140	6 670	4 750	11 505
Nigeria					40		
Peru					15		23
Philippines			15	266	635	450	953
Uruguay					97		146
Venezuela					130	650	195
Yugoslavia					50		150
Other							
Poland						150	0
Honduras				6	11		
Other						500	0
Total	762	1 330	1 601	8 967	18 278	12 000	35 121

a) Debt for equity and domestic swaps, loan-to-bond-conversions, debt repurchases and other transactions excluding interbank trading.
b) Identified to date in 1988.
Source: IMF, IECDI and DFS World Bank, Salomon Brothers, Merril Lynch, Business Latin America, International Finance Review and estimates.

principal) on existing external debt with discounted expected dividend and principal outflows associated with conversions. However, there is usually a moratorium on dividend repatriation in the initial years. Moreover, outflows from swap profits are more likely to reflect domestic economic conditions than are interest payments on debt, making the timing of profit and dividend repatriation more "bearable" and less disruptive. At the same time, from a domestic economic management perspective, it is necessary to examine the problems presented for domestic debt management, inflation, exchange rate policy, and potential foreign exchange losses through "round-tripping".

A third question is whether debt-equity swaps are a substitute for direct foreign investment or for flight capital repatriation. If they are even a partial substitute, are they the best way to attract external resources? In sum, the impact of these swaps on net resource flows must combine all these considerations – their potential size; comparison of inflows from swaps versus outflows from dividend repatriation and sale of investment; the pattern of payments and implication for debt management; and direct foreign investment and flight capital substitution. To the extent that debt-equity swaps are successful in reducing debt burden, increasing net flows, and thus improving economic conditions, creditworthiness should increase, eventually reducing future interest costs while increasing future financial flows.

Debt-equity swaps should be seen as debt relief instead of forgiveness. They offer an opportunity to reduce debt and increase equity participation. Equity participation can enhance economic structure and improve the business climate, which in time should result in better economic performance and creditworthiness. The success of Chile has shown what swaps can do. Some countries have not used them for political or economic reasons. Swaps may be unacceptable in certain developing countries since they entail a transfer from public to private ownership.

The volume of debt-for-equity swaps, though considerable, has been small relative to the total volume of outstanding debts (Table 1.5). During the period 1983-1987, external debts with a face value of $5.6 billion were retired through debt-for-equity swaps in five major user countries. Developments in 1988 increased the number of participants in the debt market. Larger banks that had refrained from selling Third World debt because of difficult accounting issues started to convert debt into equity for their own accounts, avoiding the paper losses that accompany debt sales. Debt capitalisations and conversions undertaken by domestic residents in these five countries retired an additional $1.8 billion in external debts.

Expansion of debt-equity swaps will depend on the number of countries with serious programmes, the experience of countries that already follow programmes, the development of domestic stabilization policies, and the willingness of creditors to sell their loans.

b) Debt Securitisation (Mexico-Morgan)

Morgan Guaranty Trust and the Government of Mexico made a proposal in December 1987 whereby the government offered its commercial bank creditors an opportunity to exchange Mexican loans for new Mexican government bonds, paying a higher rate of interest than on existing Mexican debt. The principal on these bonds would be collateralised by U.S. Government zero-coupon bonds purchased by Mexico[26]. The basic outline of the plan was this:

- Mexico asked for a waiver of the sharing clause from its creditors to purchase U.S. zero-coupon bonds as collateral for the Mexican bonds;

- Creditor banks sent bids to Morgan outlining how much debt they would be willing to convert for these new bonds. For example, a bank would offer to purchase a specified amount of the new Mexican bonds, such as $50 million with $100 million in existing loans, i.e. a 50 per cent discount on the existing debt.
- The Mexican government could accept or reject any bid. It obviously hoped for bids offering the largest discounts.
- When Mexico accepted a particular creditor's offer, it issued new bonds that promised to pay interest at 1⅝ per cent above six-month London Interbank Overnight Rate (LIBOR), compared to the 13/16 per cent spread above LIBOR that Mexico was committed to pay on its debt.
- Mexico was responsible for the interest payment on the bonds, and though this was higher than their original commitment, the reduced principal payment resulted in lower overall payments. A bank had the advantage of retiring some of its Mexican debt while receiving better credit for the repayment of principal. The interest payments still depend on Mexico's solvency.

The results of the Mexico-Morgan plan, announced on 4 March 1988, indicated that $3.67 billion in loans was exchanged for $2.56 billion in bonds, yielding a discount rate of about 30 per cent for the debt-to-bond conversion.

Due to the novelty of the new Mexican bond offer, originally it was difficult to value the bond to be issued on the secondary market. The bond is secured by two different credit entities (U.S. and Mexico), and each component had to be valued separately. Specifically, its principal is backed by zero-coupon U.S. Treasury bonds, whereas the interest payments carry Mexican government credit. Based on a comparable bond issue, the interest payments represent approximately 85 per cent of the bond's present value making it largely Mexican credit[27]. The discount rate applied to the principal is constant because it will remain at the risk-free rate of return for similar issues, estimated to be 8 per cent at the time. The Mexican government, on the other hand, does not enjoy the same credit rating as does the U.S. government. Therefore the interest payments should be discounted at a much higher rate (reflecting current yields on Mexican debt) to account for the higher risk. In September 1988, the market price of these new bonds was around $70.

If creditors had been convinced of its credibility, the Mexico-Morgan plan would have been more successful. Such a conviction would have, first, enhanced the value of the remaining Mexican debt held by the banks, and given its size relative to the optimistic size of the Mexico-Morgan plan, the value of the remaining debt was the critical factor in bank portfolios. Second, Mexico's improved ability to service debt would also have increased the value of the new bonds because of lower discount on the secondary market and thus a lower discount rate applied to the bond's valuation.

One could conclude that the creditors did not believe that the plan would make much difference on Mexico's creditworthiness. However, if banks had been confident of the plan's success to enhance Mexico's debt-servicing ability, they might have decided to stay on the sidelines to let other banks absorb the initial losses of the swap – this is the "free-rider" benefit.

In the wake of the Mexico-Morgan plan, variations were proposed to widen its applicability and make it more attractive to creditors.

First, many Third World countries do not have the necessary foreign exchange for the zero-coupon downpayment. So to widen the plan's scope, third parties (like international institutions or governments) could contribute grants or loans towards the initial downpayment. Second, attractiveness to creditors could be enhanced by third party guarantees of interest, interest insurance or creditor agreement to allow Mexico to treat these bonds as senior to other Mexican debt. It could be expected that an insured interest payment stream (or guarantee for a minimum interest stream within a loan/bond swap scheme such as the Mexico-Morgan Plan) would result in a lower market discount rate for the anticipated stream of coupon payments.

Although debt-equity swaps, the Mexico-Morgan plan and other such schemes may assist the menu approach, they are unlikely to provide a universal solution to the problem of Third World debt. Debt-equity swaps are limited by the availability of investment opportunities and banks' ability or willingness to sell debt at much discount; and the Mexico-Morgan plan, again, is limited by banks' willingness to swap debt.

Most importantly, if the menu approach with the above-mentioned additions does not restore the creditor banks' confidence, debtor countries will lose access to commercial credit and middle-income developing countries will become like the poorer developing countries of today, forced to rely solely on official credit, with all its negative implications for economic growth.

The argument of proponents of more comprehensive long-term measures is that sustained recovery in industrial countries, improvements in terms of trade, a drop in eurodollar interest rates, a reduction in protectionist barriers, and above all sound economic policies (including structural reform) in debtor countries can hardly be expected to occur simultaneously or for a long enough time to really ease the debt problem. The menu approach will not restore long-term debtor access to commercial credit.

So it is not surprising that, in addition to the menu approach, numerous plans have been put forward[28]. If there was a simpler, less painful solution to the debt problem, however, it would already have been adopted. There cannot be a solution with no losses. The only alternative is negotiations to determine how these losses are shared. We must rely on bilateral (or limited bilateral) negotiations, either on a country-by-country basis or within a limited group of countries. If a "solution" was found whereby creditors took substantial losses, it is uncertain that it would be in the interest of debtor countries, as they would still be barred from commercial credit. Instead, what is called for is a "positive" as opposed to zero sum approach to avoid heavy losses for banks, while debtor countries adopt the necessary policies to grow out of their economic quagmire[29].

c) Brady Plan[30]

The Brady Plan has been proposed to fill a need for debt relief. It provides this relief, which is more or less market-based, to countries that have a large financing gap and are willing to undertake a medium-term adjustment programme. For these countries, creditor banks would:

i) swap existing loans at substantial discount from bank value for newly issued long-term bonds that would carry the same spread over the LIBOR as existing loans; or
ii) swap existing loans at par for newly issued long-term bonds carrying a substantially lower interest rate (fixed or floating) than that on existing debt; or
iii) lend new money (or recycle interest payments) equivalent to a given percentage of their total exposure for a period of time.

To persuade banks to participate in debt reduction or to lend new money, the interest payments for participating banks would be guaranteed by the IMF, the World Bank and individual OECD governments for a fixed minimum time. The bonds' principal would be backed by zero-coupon U.S. treasury bonds. To attract universal participation of creditor banks, it is expected that existing loans of non-participating banks would be serviced after the bonds and loans of participating banks. This could be challenged in the courts, however, as it may contradict the normal clauses in the syndicated loan document. It is more likely that non-participating banks try to seize those countries' assets that treat bonds before loans. Although on 23 July 1989 the 15-bank steering committee for Mexico agreed to a specific package (see Chapter 4) as the first test of the Brady Plan, the agreement still required the ratification of the rest of Mexico's creditors.

Whether the Brady Plan will solve the long-term difficulties of heavier debtors and restore investments, economic growth and creditworthiness is an open question. Two factors will in large part determine its success. First, will this approach confront the realities of the debt situation? Creditors may be forced to participate but they may also permanently withdraw commercial credit for most developing countries. The second determinant is whether the IMF, the World Bank and the OECD governments will allocate enough resources to reach satisfactory agreements for all problem debtor countries[31].

Realities of a Solution

There have been laudable attempts to solve debt problems: better adjustment policies, rescheduling, additional flows from the World Bank, debt-equity swaps and most recently, the Brady Plan. Nevertheless, economic performance in major debtor countries remains unsatisfactory, with low economic growth and investment ratios[32]. The longer the debt situation persists, the higher the price paid by developing countries.

Any realistic initiative to ease the Third World debt problem must create a balance between the interests of creditors and debtors. This balance includes the varied financial conditions of creditor institutions, accounting and tax regulations and economic and political realities in creditor countries, the free-rider issue, debt relief that promotes acceptable debtor growth, economic and political realities in debtor countries and flight capital.

a) Financial Condition of Creditors

Some creditor institutions have been weakened by the non-performance of a substantial portion of their Third World loans. Other factors, as well, have contributed to their financial difficulties. Deregulation of financial markets and the resulting competition have increased their funding costs. With a lowered financial rating and better opportunities for non-bank financing of highly-rated corporations, disintermediation has occurred, and they have lost some of their traditional lending business to prime corporate borrowers. The latter have been able to satisfy their financing requirements more cheaply and more flexibly from banking and non-banking institutions because of note issuance facilities (NIFs), commercial paper, euro-commercial paper, bonds, swaps and euro-equities[33]. These developments have further diminished the quality of bank assets and balance sheets.

Regulators in several countries mandated increased capital-asset ratio requirements to try to help the commercial banks. The banks then turned to off-balance-sheet activities – NIFs and swaps, for example – to improve their earnings. Bank regulators next adopted a weighted risk asset approach to capital adequacy (to be phased in by 1992), as opposed to a straight capital-to-asset ratio[34]. This weighted approach was meant to improve capital adequacy by incorporating what are currently considered off-balance-sheet items. At the

Table 1.6. LOAN LOSS RESERVES AGAINST THIRD WORLD DEBT IN CREDITOR COUNTRIES

End 1987

Belgium	– Average 31.5%, range 20-50% LDC coverage
Canada	– 39.3% average coverage
France	– 40-45% average coverage
Germany	– at least 40% coverage
Italy	– 4.5% coverage
Japan	– 10% coverage
Luxembourg	– 41-45% coverage
Netherlands	– 35% coverage
Sweden	– 61% coverage (1986)
Switzerland	– 60% coverage
U.K.	– average 30% coverage, included trade debt

Source: "Report to Governors", Committee on Banking Regulations and Supervisory Practices, Bank for International Settlement, Basle, Switzerland, Draft, March 29, 1988.

same time, commercial banks have responded to market and non-market forces by recognising the quality problem of their Third World loans and increasing loan loss provisioning (see Table 1.6)[35].

The impact of these developments has varied. First, the relative exposure to capital of commercial banks in different creditor countries, especially to problem debt, has been

Table 1.7. BALANCE OF PRIVATE BANKS' LOANS TO CENTRAL AND SOUTH AMERICAN DEBTOR COUNTRIES

$ 100 million, October 1986

Home country of bank	United States	Japan	U.K.	France	Germany	Canada	Total[1]
Debtor Country							
Brazil	237	82	91	84	63	56	613
Mexico	242	100	87	55	38	55	577
Argentina	77	43	37	19	33	14	222
Venezuela	47	37	27	25	21	21	177
Chile	63	14	22	6	10	10	125
Ecuador	50	7	8	2	3	3	73
Colombia	23	10	8	6	5	5	56
Peru	14	4	6	7	5	1	38
Uruguay	9	1	4	1	1	1	16
Bolivia	1	–	1	1	1	1	5
Total	763	298	291	206	180	167	1 902
Percentage	40.0	15.6	15.2	10.8	9.5	8.7	100

1. Figures rounded down to the nearest million.
Source: Ninon keizai Shimbun, Estimation of International Financial Sources, May 21, 1987. Translated from Japanese.

irregular (see Table 1.7). In most countries debt exposure is concentrated in a few international banks. Second, different accounting and tax treatments in creditor countries produce dissimilar bank balance sheets and income statements. Third, the depreciation of the dollar since 1985 has favoured non-dollar-based banks, where the domestic currency value of Third World loans has declined. For dollar-based banks they have remained constant[36]. (Commercial Third World loans have been booked largely in dollars.) Fourth, because of additional capital requirements, U.S. banks have been at a disadvantage compared to banks in countries like Japan where the equity markets have been strong or price-earning ratios high.

b) Accounting and Tax Regulations in Creditor Countries

Accounting principles and tax regulations affect the ability of commercial banks to manage their problem loans[37]. Accounting methods could indicate that a swap (at a realised discount) of part of a country's debt would result in increased provisioning for the remaining portion that the bank continued to hold. Alternatively, the swap could result in the remaining portion of the country's debt (or even of similar categorised countries) having to be written down (contamination effect). The most favourable interpretation would consist of only realised losses being recognised. In the case of debt-debt swaps in which banks swap one country's debt for another's to rearrange their portfolios, losses are not generally realised if there is a $1 for $1 face-value swap. However, if one debt is selling for 80 cents on the dollar and the other 40 cents, a two-for-one swap could result in a realised loss of 50 cents *only* on the lower-rated debt; this is because the bank avoids recognising that *both* are at a discount in a direct debt-for-debt swap.

A second important difference in the effect of regulations concerns loan-loss provisioning; the ability to make the provisions, whether they can be included in bank capital, and the tax treatment afforded them. Some countries have mandatory provisioning for problem countries (identified by regulators), while others do not.

A third effect of accounting and tax regulation is the treatment of interest capitalisation schemes. The questions are: Should accrued interest be taxed in the current period? Should capitalised interest be taxed as received interest at the time of the capitalisation, at the time of repayment of the capitalised interest, or over the life of capitalisation? Should it be counted as new exposure requiring additional reserves? And should capitalisation be grounds for placing a loan on a nonaccrued basis?

As a result of differing accounting and tax treatment and the position taken by regulators (capital-to-asset ratios and mandatory provisioning for selected debt), the ability of creditor banks to manage their Third World debt exposure has been uneven. While affecting the ability to manage losses, accounting and tax treatment has not influenced a bank's perception of a country's creditworthiness. Both because of major national differences and its unfavourableness in certain major creditor countries, this treatment has made universal participation in resolving the debt problem unlikely. The adoption of looser, more uniform tax and accounting methods would help.

Specific provisions that U.S. banks would appreciate include: tax-deductible reserves (preferably for a group of countries), more liberal rules for loss recognition, tax deductibility for partial losses, and more flexibility in valuations of debt swaps. Canadian and Swiss banks are generally happy with their national treatment. Japanese banks are faced with adverse contamination effects, as any losses on swaps must be translated into a write-down of the balance of the country's loan they continue to hold. They also face disadvantageous tax treatment in the accounting of these losses. Moreover they are not free to provision beyond 10 per cent of face value.

Unifying accounting and tax handling is by no means an easy task. It would, however, allow banks to participate more in the menu approach and any other new scheme. After the success of the Basle agreement in harmonizing the definition of capital and capital-asset ratios, the next step should be co-ordination of asset valuation and then accounting and tax treatment. While it may be unrealistic to expect results soon, these are desirable goals for the international community.

c) Free-Rider Issue

Proposed solutions to the Third World debt crisis must come to terms with the free-rider issue.

Naturally a commercial bank would prefer other banks to take the initiative to solve debt problems while it benefits from the debtor country's improved debt-servicing ability. If commercial banks are asked to participate in 50 per cent debt forgiveness on a voluntary basis, then no bank will want to make the first step and incur the losses inherent in debt forgiveness.

The free-rider issue has been a source of delay in the provision of new credits under reschedulings. A non-contributing bank could benefit from higher interest payments on its existing loans and might stand to gain further if loan values increased. The free-rider issue has even wider implications; when commercial loans are rescheduled, international institutions also get a "free ride".

The problem is much the same in the case of debt relief. The only difference is that instead of new credits, the sharing of losses may be made more difficult by unfavourable tax and accounting treatments.

Any proposal should therefore envisage creditor banks' participation on a proportional (to outstanding Third World debt) basis, much the same as in reschedulings.

d) Economic and Political Realities in Creditor Countries

Any solution based on creditor country governments and/or international institutions absorbing all losses – buying the bulk of the loans or guaranteeing the bulk of the debt-servicing – is unworkable in the present environment. Budgetary constraints in some major creditor countries and the perception of imprudent bank lending would make an official bail-out unlikely. Only if disaster struck first would a bail-out occur, probably never as a preventive measure.

In the United States, severe budgetary deficits during the 1980s resulted in mandatory cutbacks in government deficit spending (Gramm-Rudman). A direct or indirect official bail-out would be unpopular, forcing cutbacks in domestic programmes that have already been squeezed. The U.S. regulators will bail out banks if they have to, but on a case-by-case basis and only after relating its cost to that of government deposit insurance, in case the bank was allowed to go into bankruptcy. None of this would help Third World debtors.

Although the economy has performed well in Japan, budgetary deficits have been a historical problem there. Basically, Japanese banks do not have as large an exposure (relative to total Third World debt or assets) to Latin American countries as U.S. banks do; so an official bail-out is not as necessary. Within the Brady Plan, however, Japan has been ready to contribute substantial funding.

In Europe, only three countries – the United Kingdom, France and the Federal Republic of Germany – have significant exposure to some problem debtors in Latin America. France has some of the same problems as the United States. The United Kingdom's current budgetary difficulties are less severe that those of the United States, and the FRG, which has fewer budgetary difficulties than any other European country, is more concerned with their East European exposure.

e) Sufficient Debt Relief

Any realistic solution to Third World debt must include sufficient debt relief. Sufficient relief would put the debtor country on the road to acceptable and sustained economic growth, restoring creditworthiness and commercial credit access. Here we assume that the country also does its part by adopting good policies.

Calculations of sufficient debt relief should consider several factors. Estimates should incorporate a range of possible interest rates for debt-servicing. Economic structure, commodity prices, world economic growth and protectionism all should be weighed. An estimate of sufficient debt relief agreed to by both debtors and creditors is indispensable. For creditors, sufficent debt relief is defined as restoration of value to bank assets. If a scheme lacks enough relief to restore increased value to the part of debt they would continue to hold, its attractiveness to creditors is reduced. Krugman has made this point very elegantly[38]. Market solutions are said to be workable if they enhance a creditor's overall financial position. Sufficient debt relief for debtors is defined as enough savings (plus external loans) to enable them to grow at satisfactory rates while servicing the new level of debt and the required level of investments. For them, sufficient debt relief would more likely induce appropriate adjustment policies. Governments of industrial countries and international institutions view sufficient debt relief as debtors' restored access to commercial credit, enhancement of growth prospects and political stability. Calculations show that about a 40 per cent reduction in debt-servicing obligation may be required; this estimate is an average for countries in the Baker Plan and is based on the size of commercial debt prevailing at the end of 1987.

f) Economic and Political Realities in Debtor Countries

Many debtor countries have experienced dismal economic performance. Real economic growth has been low resulting in negative *per capita* income growth. Investment to GNP ratios have declined or at best have remained constant in many countries, with consumption providing the basis for growth. When countries have had a substantial trade surplus, it has been used to finance debt-servicing, resulting in a net outflow of funds[39]. These symptoms have been accompanied by deep-seated problems such as high inflation, budget deficits and structural distortions. The interest on external debt has been itself a major cause of budget deficits, creating further inflationary pressures and demanding monetary and fiscal tightening. Economic difficulties invariably result in political polarisation with everyone calling for a painless solution to the debt problem while promising improvements in the standard of living.

From the debtor point of view a proposal to address Third World debt must include more resources for economic growth and development than currently available. This can be achieved through any of the following:

i) reduction in the size of debt,
ii) reduction in interest payments (either because of reduced debt, lower interest rates or interest capitalisation),
iii) tying debt-servicing to some acceptable measure of a country's ability to service debt, and
iv) new lending.

Without these incentives, debtor countries will have little reason to service their debt.

g) Flight Capital

While many Third World countries have seen their external debt grow over the last fifteen years, the assets of their citizens abroad in the form of flight capital and other investments have grown by leaps and bounds. Creditor institutions would like to see some of this capital repatriated; from their perspective, it is difficult to remain engaged in Third World lending when citizens have no confidence in their own economies.

There have been large capital outflows exacerbating foreign exchange shortages in a number of developing countries (Argentina, Mexico, Venezuela and others). Even a partial reversal of capital flight could improve the international position of debtor nations and broaden the possibilities for easing the debt crisis[40].

Capital flight is hard to measure, though a variety of estimation methods exists. In Table 1.8 calculations of capital flight for six countries are presented. As the figures indicate, these countries' estimates are large, even though they undervalue today's stock of flight capital in at least two ways:

1. the figures do not reflect more recent years; and
2. the figures do not include historic interest, dividends, or capital appreciation.

Flight capital is so important in total Third World debt, the question must be asked: How can debtor countries contain, even induce a return of flight capital to their countries? There are several policies debtor countries can follow, but political stability may be the overriding factor.

First, macro-economic policy must inspire public confidence. Vital to success are *a)* setting a realistic exchange rate, *b)* maintaining a positive but moderate interest rate, *c)* encouraging strong economic growth, and *d)* favouring a medium-term resolution of the debt problem. Far-reaching economic growth is probably the most important single deterrent to capital flight because it restores confidence in the domestic economy and opens new investment opportunities.

Second, debtor countries must reduce corruption by ending the rationing of underpriced foreign exchange or credit.

Third, countries should improve domestic financial intermediation by broadening and deepening markets. This can be accomplished by:

1. strengthening the capital base of the financial sector;
2. improving bank regulation; and
3. increasing the role of bond and equity financing [41].

Fourth, exchange controls can be effective as a complement to (rather than a substitute for) sound macro-economic policies. Relatively modest capital outflows from Brazil, Chile, Colombia and Peru at the turn of the decade support this conclusion. These countries

Table 1.8. CAPITAL FLIGHT ESTIMATE

Average in millions of dollars

	1976	1977	1978	1979	1980	1981	1982	1983	1984	1976-84
Argentina	108	466	1 814	1 686	3 960	6 160	7 487	1 994	(2 994)	20 889
Brazil	(378)	3 244	1 272	745	1 727	(515)	1 830	812	3 366	12 105
South Korea	127	559	818	(167)	(362)	87	1 090	88	604	2 844
Mexico	3 445	3 597	872	1 269	5 235	7 568	6 708	9 250	4 251	42 192
Philippines	726	840	429	367	397	1 531	609	(750)	(1 031)	3 114
Venezuela	(3 443)	1 194	698	2 561	5 412	5 826	4 649	3 111	4 016	24 021

Source: *Robert Comby and Richard Levich, "On the Definition and Magnitude of Recent Capital Flight", in Capital Flight and Third World Debt,* ed. Donald R. Lessard and John Williamson, (Washington, D.C.: Institute for International Economics, 1987), Statistical Annex A, pp. 52-63.

maintained restrictions on capital outflows, while Argentina, Mexico and Venezuela did not.

Finally, countries experiencing capital flight need to remove tax incentives to invest funds abroad rather than at home.

h) Balance Between Creditor and Debtor Interests

The interest spreads and the economies of scale associated with Third World lending in the 1970s made it very profitable. When appropriately determined, the spreads were a compensation for risk. It therefore seems fitting that banks realise some of the risk or costs in view of their past profits. While banks should agree to accept some losses, they cannot be expected to endorse solutions like total debt forgiveness that could erode their entire capital base. Normally, banks can be expected only to embrace solutions that enhance their present position[42].

The debtors must also bear responsibility for economic mismanagement. Debt moratoria, though possibly helpful in the very short run, are eventually counter-productive. Debtors cannot be expected to accept solutions like more resource outflow and ultimately lower *per capita* incomes and growth that are below the *status quo,* but they should appreciate that a zero sum solution in their favour would be against their long-term interests if they lost commercial credit access.

Creditor governments should also help resolve the debt problem because of the potential benefits to the world economy and to political stability in the Third World. Additionally, if losses are suffered by commercial lenders, official creditor governments in industrial countries should expect to suffer a proportionate loss on their official loans.

Basis of a Solution

Since the onset of the debt crisis in 1982, and with increasing frequency in recent years, new solutions to the Third World debt problem have surfaced. Many, if not most, have incorporated some form of financial innovation. Unfortunately, innovations cannot magically offer debt relief. Debt relief may be simply a zero sum game that is made palatable by financial innovations. However, to the extent that debt relief ultimately results in more favourable global, political and economic performance, all parties may benefit over and above their initial concessions. To be beneficial to all parties, debt relief must increase the size of the "pie", and this can be accomplished in various ways:

i) Enhanced adjustment policies by debtors: lower debt service, increased conditionality, and conditional debt-servicing based on variables outside a debtor's control (such as export prices);

ii) Tax and accounting changes in creditor countries to improve the balance sheet and income statement of creditor banks;

iii) Third party funds in the form of guarantees or direct contributors.

There are several innovations that individually or combined can afford some debt relief: discount on the secondary market for debt, swaps, options, futures, debt subordination, interest capitalisation, and conditioned debt-servicing. Unfortunately most of these solutions do not pay enough attention to economic and political realities or take sufficient advantage of existing opportunities.

a) Secondary Market Discount

In the last three or four years, an increasingly active secondary market has developed[43] where Third World debt can be sold at a substantial discount. Because of this, debt could potentially be retired at a fraction of its face value. One can only say potentially because this market is still very "thin" and it is uncertain how much of the debt can be purchased at, or near, existing discounts. In particular, if large amounts of debt are purchased, the discount may shrink dramatically[44]. This is partly because buying debt on the secondary market to afford debt relief to debtors (through a scheme like the Mexico-Morgan Plan), would benefit the holder (as opposed to sellers) by increasing the debt's value. This is an outcome of the debtor's improved ability to meet debt service payments (the free-rider issue). Another reason for the thinness of this market is the financial difficulties associated with asset contamination following the sale of debt; this has meant that large instead of small holders have not been selling. Closely connected is the fact that, given their existing exposure levels, many banks cannot easily absorb the losses associated with asset contamination.

Although discussions with market participants indicate that secondary market prices are meaningless, at least for any sizeable transaction, some banks (mostly those with small Third World debt exposure) are willing to take a loss. This is a marked change of attitude from 1982, when banks would not even consider the possibility. Today, some banks absorb losses to eliminate their exposure, and even bigger banks quietly appear to be open to a "serious" global proposal that could result in substantial losses, though not at current secondary market prices.

To reap the benefit of these discounts, the supply curve for Third World debt should be determined. This supply depends on: extent of individual creditor exposure, financial viability of individual creditors, accounting and tax regulations, level of write-offs and loan-loss provisions and the impact of debt retirement on the debtor's ability to service debt. Any plan to incorporate discount benefits (substantial debt purchase as opposed to marginal) must consider the free-rider issue. This means that creditors must be persuaded to sell a portion of their Third World debt at a fixed discount to avoid marginal purchases producing increasingly smaller discounts. More importantly, creditors must be convinced of the viability of debtors to stay engaged in the restoration of long-term commercial access.

Benefits from debt purchase may be enhanced if debt sale is supported by economic policy reforms in debtor countries (through IMF/World Bank). Because creditors benefit from the portion of the debt not sold, they would more readily agree to take a bigger loss on a debt's sale if it improved the debtor country's chances of meeting its future debt-service payments, thus increasing the value of the unsold debt. In this sense, there is a distinct role for a more aggressive IMF and World Bank as intermediaries or enforcers, not necessarily as guarantors or providers of funds. However, if the IMF and the World Bank were to act as enforcers, they would have to be more active in ensuring strong policies in debtor countries.

Another assessment of debt relief resulting from the purchase of debt on the secondary market is the way in which a purchase plan uses the discount to benefit the debtor country. The full discount could reduce the debt and the interest rate could be maintained at its original level, thus reducing the size of debt-service payments. Alternatively, debt size could be reduced and the interest rate increased (affording the debtor less debt relief), or the debt could remain the same while interest rates were cut.

These schemes could suggest the purchase of the debt by a new or existing institution like IMF or World Bank. The purchase could be financed by issuing new instruments to the banks, with the interest passed on from the debtor country; this interest could be guaranteed or not guaranteed, with implications for the debt's purchase price. The debt could also be bought by the debtor country through a swap for a new instrument issued by the debtor.

The important point is that banks may now be willing, under appropriate conditions, to realise some losses on their Third World loans, and this willingness could entail smaller debt-service payments. At the same time, the discount on Third World debt should not be used as a giant exit bond. This would destroy commercial creditors' confidence in Third World countries.

b) Swaps and Buy-backs

Swaps, swapping debt for another asset, can be also used in debt relief. Debt can be directly swapped for a real asset in a debtor country, with or without a discount on the debt, thus reducing interest payments.

Debt-equity swaps have been the most frequently used. Usually the debt has not been directly swapped for equity by the original holder. Instead, a third party bought the debt at discount and swapped it for an asset in the debtor country, usually within a debtor country's debt-equity swap programme. The potential contribution of these swaps to debt relief was discussed earlier; they should not be seen solely as relief, but as a way to promote structural change, improve economic performance, and enhance the business climate. Again, debt-equity swaps (made viable because of discount on sale of debt) are unlikely to singlehandedly solve the debt problem, but their role could be expanded to assist more countries' programmes.

Swaps can be also used in the exchange of existing loans for new bonds (at a discount from face value or carrying a lower interest rate). The Mexico-Morgan plan was one such application. To afford debt relief, though, interest guarantees by credible third parties are almost a necessity.

Debt buy-backs by debtor countries are yet another form of swap – cash for loans. Such a calculation must take into account that the current large discounts on Third World debt are a signal that the market does not expect debt to be fully serviced; the suitable alternative is less than full debt-service.

c) Options and Futures

Options and futures on Third World debt may be used to reduce the risk for holders. Options and futures would allow banks to hedge their long cash-market position by offsetting futures positions, while investors could hedge their cash-market exposure by an offsetting position in the futures market. Banks would charge higher prices that include a premium, compensating for the risks involved in falling debt market prices (which have lately been the norm) on the balance of their loan assets. However, it would be difficult to ascertain *a priori* the extent to which these contracts would be used by hedgers or speculators since such a market might be too thin.

Options and futures can be used as a part of the menu approach. In a speech in London in May, 1988, the former treasurer of the World Bank, Mr. Rotberg, suggested some interesting applications. To encourage new lending by banks, he suggested that they buy a "put option" (from the World Bank) to convert their new loans at maturity into a U.S. government security. This would safeguard their loan principal and encourage new lending.

The use of options and futures on Third World debt would improve the efficiency of its secondary market. This in turn would improve the viability of debt-swaps and other schemes that rely on market discounts.

d) Debt Subordination

To encourage new lending to Third World countries, outstanding debt could be subordinated to new debt. This suggestion cannot stand on its own since it would be at the expense of existing creditors and naturally would be rejected by them. Nevertheless it is possible that in the context of an overall plan, debt subordination could play a useful role. Specifically creditor governments could subordinate their lending to commercial lending to stimulate more commercial loans.

e) Interest Capitalisation

Debt relief in the form of capitalised interest enlarges the debtor country's cash flow by reducing the interest paid in the current period. It can also be used as an alternative to new money flows. It can help when debt-servicing is a short- to medium-term, not a long-term, problem. Deferring repayments, however, creates future servicing difficulties, possibly even more onerous than if good policy measures had been taken in the first place. Another criticism of this approach has targeted the lack of incentive for economic discipline to improve domestic policies. Bankers especially dislike interest capitalisation both because of accounting and tax problems and because it implies a departure from market pricing, giving the wrong signals to debtors.

Again, however, interest capitalisation, though unacceptable in itself may have a role in a wide-ranging solution when coupled with IMF conditionality.

f) Conditional debt-servicing

The tying of debt-service payments to export performance of debtor countries has also been done. The attractions of this idea are its closer approximation of a country's ability to pay and its incentives to countries to adopt appropriate policies through advantageous export prices[45]. In private conversations, bankers have indicated their openness to such proposals if the appropriate criteria are used *and* if the ability to pay is symmetrical – that is, flexible both up and down, not merely in one direction. An additional request was made that loans be collateralised by commodities or third party guarantees that the debtor's new obligations will be honoured. It is unlikely that any such scheme alone could restore growth in developing countries. It could ameliorate short-run financial constraints but may not provide sufficient long-term debt relief to revive acceptable economic performance, unless creditor banks were willing to take a generous position on the relationship of export prices to debt-servicing obligations.

Direction of a Solution

The key objectives for all debtor countries is increased net financial flows (new inflows or reduction in existing outflow of obligations) and improved creditworthiness. The commercial creditors' objective is a solution they can "afford" in terms of capital, and an improvement in their financial condition (while not expecting total resolution of the problems). Official creditors, OECD governments and international and regional institutions, along with commercial creditors, would like to enhance financial conditions in Third World countries and ensure continued access to commercial credit; if Third World countries lose long-term access, official creditors cannot, or will not, fill the void. The focus of this discussion is not official creditors and their debtors. Nevertheless, a few words are necessary in their regard.

Creditor governments have usually chosen for political reasons to ignore the existence of problem loans. In many cases governments cannot by law forgive debt and, practically speaking, it is difficult to acquire real assets in debtor countries. A large proportion of official loans goes to countries that cannot pay either now or later. Therefore official loans are a separate, political issue and cannot be addressed with fundamentally market-oriented solutions. However, official creditors are also exposed to the debtors in the Baker fifteen and other countries that have incurred mostly commercial debt. Borrowings from governments have been largely treated as senior to commercial debt in these countries. Commercial creditors might think it only reasonable that official creditors participate (i.e. absorb losses) to the same extent or proportion as they[46].

For Third World debt, the essence of proposed solutions (in the absence of outright debt forgiveness) is the best way to take advantage of discounts on the market and banks' acceptance of a discount (negotiation), since the secondary market may not reflect actual willingness. This brings up two questions:

a) how should Third World debt be acquired from creditors? The answer to this should consider the realities of the debt situation discussed above and, more importantly, the debt purchase should be at a negotiated discount.

b) what should be done with the debt once it is acquired? Again this answer should be realistic, but it is here that imagination, innovations and plans come into play.

As we have said, a large purchase of Third World debt on the secondary market may substantially reduce the size of discounts. Third World debt should be bought at a negotiated price simultaneously from all creditor banks in a market-oriented plan to realise a fair discount, avoid giving "free-rider" benefits to some creditors and keep commercial banks involved in the debt process. This approach has the additional benefit of restoring creditors' confidence, and if the sale of some of the debt enhances the value of the remaining portion they continue to hold, they will be more amenable to selling at a discount and reopening access to credit.

Another question in debt acquisition is how the entity (new institution, IMF, World Bank) should pay for it. There are various options – cash; a new instrument to be issued by the acquiring institution; or an instrument to be issued by the debtor country with third party guarantees (interest and/or principal). For a creditor, the more guarantees the better. If no guarantees are given, with the interest simply passed through to creditors, then creditors must at least be convinced that the debtor's ability to service its remaining debt has really improved, i.e. "sufficient" debt relief. At the other extreme, either payment is in cash, better credit is substituted for the Third World debtor's credit, or the interest and principal are guaranteed by a better credit.

The issue arises of what per cent of the realised discount should be passed on the debtor country. If all of it is transferred, leverage with the debtor decreases. If some of the discount is kept by the acquiring intermediary institution, the interest from that portion could be used to build up reserves against future debtor non-performance. These reserves could support guarantees and safeguard the creditors' interests in the absence of official guarantees.

Related to this is the best use of discount benefits in the context of conditionality. Conditionality, necessary to any debtor commitment to safeguard creditor interests, should be viewed in a long-term framework to emphasize economic growth and ensure open markets for debtor country exports with the help of IMF surveillance. In this context, even partial IMF/World Bank guarantees would contribute to the recovery of creditor confidence.

These are the basic opportunities offered by the discount that can be obtained on debt acquisition.

Any approach would be assisted by the following measures:

i) more favourable accounting and tax treatment of debt transactions (sale, swap, loan-loss provisioning) for commercial banks and an eventual standardisation throughout countries;

ii) agreement by government creditors not to have the Third World credits treated *de facto* as senior to commercial credits and to make concessions on their Third World loans;

iii) realistic proposals for tying of debt-servicing to export earnings capacity, heightening debtors' incentives for economic restructuring;

iv) economic co-operation by creditors to improve their own countries' economic performance, improve market access for Third World exports and adopt a unified approach to the debt problem;

v) better management of domestic economic policies in debtor countries to increase growth, productivity, the ability to service debt and consequently reverse capital flight.

The essence of our argument for a more general solution than the menu approach is clear. With enough realistic commitment the problem of Third World debt could be corrected to restore the confidence of commercial creditors in much of the Third World, restore growth and access to credit there, and strengthen creditors' long-term position.

a) Application of Secondary Market Discounts

An international institution like the World Bank could:

i) buy Third World debt from stronger banks at a negotiated level of discount; this could be even lower that the currently available market discount (these loans take a smaller percentage of their capital than three years ago because of the depreciation of the dollar), motivating banks to participate;

ii) in exchange for Third World debt, the World Bank could issue bonds denominated in the banks' own currency (Yen, DM, etc.) taking advantage of these currencies' low coupon and eliminating banks' foreign exchange exposure;

iii) the World Bank could pass on the benefits (some or all) of the discount, the lower interest rate on the World Bank bonds and the lower coupon rate of the stronger currency, to the debtor country;

iv) the debtor country would have to agree to appropriate conditionality.

Such a plan would have to lower debt-service payment enough to induce growth in debtor countries. As a further incentive debt-servicing could be symmetrically tied to export performance.

b) Variants without Institutional Credit Support

In the above general solution, we suggested that the purchase of Third World debt be accompanied by some substitution of international institutional credit for debtor's credit. If banks took a loss on the swap of a portion of Third World debt, they would certainly want institutional guarantees to enhance the value of the debt that they continue to hold. However, if creditors were convinced of fundamental economic policy changes like structural reform and a debtor's ability to service its debt, then third party guarantees, though useful, may not be necessary.

c) Measures to Broaden Holding of Debt

Futures and options on Third World debt could be instituted to improve market efficiency and broaden the holding of debt to non-bank investors.

d) Government Contributions to Debt Swaps

Governments of countries with creditor banks would agree to contribute so that their banks swap at a discount an agreed amount of debt (proportional to their debt holding) for new debt. The premise of such a plan would be:

i) to give some debt relief;

ii) if banks swapped, for example, 50 per cent of their debt and took the loss, the full value of the other 50 per cent of the debt (the interest on which could be guaranteed) would result in a much stronger balance sheet than the current one. (If the discount is currently 50 per cent, the market value of $1 of debt is $0.5, if banks believe that secondary market valuations are correct; but with the proposed swap it would be $0.5 + $0.25 = $0.75);

iii) many variants on such a plan could be improvised as long as they provide sufficient debt relief and motivate creditor banks by enhancing their future balance sheet (through, for example, partial official guarantees on interest).

It is essential for the four major participants – creditor countries, international institutions, commercial creditors and debtor countries – to make their commitments known and adopt a co-ordinated approach. Co-ordination is made more difficult by the numerous parties involved, but without it a solution is impossible.

Conclusion

Problem Third World debt has had, and will continue to have, negative economic and political consequences for creditors and debtors, as well as for the entire world.

At first the debt crisis was seen as a short-term liquidity problem. More recently it has been seen as a global predicament, affecting not just heavily indebted nations but the international economic system. Although the menu approach may have somewhat ameliorated debt-servicing problems, economic performance in Third World countries remains unsatisfactory. For many of the distressed commercial debtor countries, sustained economic recovery in industrial countries, reduced real interest rates and protectionism, and most importantly appropriate domestic economic policies, are required to restore economic growth and improve creditworthiness. Many plans have been proposed to develop and maintain these desirable conditions.

These plans have received little support from creditor institutions and governments. Most projects envisage only debt relief in the context of a zero sum game, not only lacking creditor support but possibly detrimental to debtors in the long run, cutting off their access to commercial credit. Other plans involve a turn-around in debtor policies but still receive little encouragement from either creditors or debtors.

Some new directions exist. Since creditors are now potentially willing to absorb discounts on Third World debt, it is possible to construct a less painful solution. A new approach would have to be far-reaching and realistic, but above all it must secure the commitment of creditor and debtor governments and creditor institutions. Debtors must incorporate reforms and policies that restore creditor confidence. Without this confidence, the problems could become insurmountable. As commercially indebted Third World countries lose market access, their inadequate growth will have negative implications for the global economy. The essence of the Brady Plan – debt reduction – tries to prevent this, though perhaps within a vacuum of too little assessment of the debt situation from the perspective of both creditors and debtors.

CHILE'S AND MEXICO'S EXTERNAL DEBT

Introduction

These two countries' external debt, like that of other major debtors, has increased substantially since 1975. The increased availability of external financial resources (other things being equal) theoretically should have improved economic performance in both countries, but adverse external developments and mismanaged macro-economic adjustment policies have negated their potentially positive contributions. This study analyses economic developments in Chile and Mexico to shed some light on their current external debt management. It also examines both countries' future prospects and attempts to draw conclusions that may apply to other heavily indebted countries.

External Debt Developments

Chile

Chile's external debt increased sharply between 1975 and 1987 (see Table 1.9). During this period total external debt rose from $4 854 million to $19 208 million, while medium- and long-term debt went from $4 267 million to $17 191 million (the increase was strongest in 1979). External shocks and internal policy developments fuelled the borrowing, especially within the private sector. In Chile during this period there was some voluntary lending from commercial banks – when other heavily indebted countries had bad ratios of interest payments to export earnings, Chile's was very favourable. Debt rescheduling for Chile is not a problem because of the confidence the banks have in the country. This initial concentration of external debt in the private sector is unique among heavily indebted Latin American countries.

Although external indebtedness rose dramatically between 1979 and 1982, it was not reflected as a permanent increase in fixed investment. Investment as a percentage of GDP was lower in 1982 than it was in the years before 1979. Investment averaged 16 per cent of GDP over 1974-1976, 14 per cent over 1977-1978, 14.9 per cent in 1979, 16.6 per cent in 1980 and 18.5 per cent in 1981, then declined to 13.8 per cent in 1982[47].

Heavy external borrowing is reflected in a variety of debt ratios (see Table 1.10). Total external debt to exports of goods and services increased from 192.5 per cent in 1980 to 436.7 per cent in 1985, falling to 327.4 per cent in 1987; total external debt to GNP increased from 45.3 per cent in 1980 to 144.4 per cent, falling to 124.1 per cent in 1987; and the debt-service ratio rose from 21.9 per cent in 1980 to 29.6 per cent in 1981, and stood at 21.1 per cent in 1987.

The recent slight decline in Chile's external debt demonstrates the impact of narrowing current account deficits and debt conversions (see Chapter 2). Private debt has decreased,

Table 1.9. CHILE'S EXTERNAL DEBT 1975-1987*

Millions of US$ at end of each year

	1975	1976	1977	1978	1979	1980	1981	1982	1983	1984	1985	1986	1987
I. Total external debt (II+III)	**4 854**	**4 720**	**5 201**	**6 664**	**8 484**	**11 084**	**15 542**	**17 153**	**17 431**	**18 877**	**19 444**	**19 501**	**19 208**
Public Sector	4 068	3 762	3 917	4 709	5 063	5 063	5 465	6 660	9 795	12 343	14 079	15 763	16 380
Public Financial Sector	736	638	635	1 062	1 349	1 261	925	1 615	3 254	5 058	5 713	5 725	6 001
Banco del Estado	(166)	(121)	(94)	(274)	(252)	(314)	(397)	(778)	(877)	(1 386)	(1 356)	(1 296)	(1 078)
Central Bank	(570)	(517)	(541)	(788)	(1 097)	(947)	(528)	(837)	(2 377)	(3 672)	(4 357)	(4 429)	(4 923)
Public non-financial Sector	3 311	3 094	3 236	3 599	3 638	3 730	4 471	4 983	4 726	5 155	6 018	6 630	7 103
Treasury	(1 656)	(1 615)	(1 550)	(1 491)	(1 287)	(1 196)	(1 068)	(1 133)	(1 129)	(1 276)	(1 990)	(2 614)	(2 993)
Others	(1 655)	(1 479)	(1 686)	(2 108)	(2 351)	(2 534)	(3 403)	(3 850)	(3 597)	(3 879)	(4 028)	(4 016)	(4 110)
Private Sector with Public Guarantee	21	30	46	48	76	72	69	62	1 815	2 130	2 348	3 408	3 276
Private Sector	786	958	1 264	1 955	3 421	6 021	10 077	10 493	7 636	6 534	5 365	3 738	2 828
Banks and Financial Institutions	(154)	(168)	(309)	(660)	(1 453)	(3 497)	(6 629)	(6 703)	(4 195)	(3 469)	(2 786)	(1 463)	(737)
Corporate and Private Debtors[1]	(632)	(790)	(975)	(1 295)	(1 968)	(2 524)	(3 448)	(3 790)	(3 441)	(3 065)	(2 579)	(2 275)	(2 091)
II. Medium- and long-term external debt	**4 267**	**4 274**	**4 510**	**5 923**	**7 507**	**9 413**	**12 553**	**13 815**	**14 832**	**16 963**	**17 650**	**17 814**	**17 191**
Public Sector	3 597	3 475	3 520	4 353	4 771	4 720	4 415	5 157	8 090	10 601	12 515	14 379	14 725
Public Financial Sector	451	541	560	904	1 340	1 257	921	1 144	2 686	4 464	5 269	5 608	5 749
Banco del Estado	(14)	(24)	(24)	(121)	(243)	(310)	(393)	(507)	(609)	(1 272)	(1 237)	(1 179)	(1 051)
Central Bank	(437)	(517)	(536)	(783)	(1 097)	(947)	(528)	(637)	(2 077)	(3 192)	(4 032)	(4 429)	(4 698)
Public non-financial Sector	3 125	2 904	2 914	3 401	3 355	3 391	3 425	3 951	3 941	4 419	5 245	5 836	6 302
Treasury	(1 656)	(1 615)	(1 550)	(1 491)	(1 287)	(1 196)	(1 068)	(1 109)	(1 105)	(1 276)	(1 990)	(2 614)	(2 993)
Others	(1 469)	(1 289)	(1 364)	(1 910)	(2 068)	(2 195)	(2 357)	(2 842)	(2 836)	(3 143)	(3 255)	(3 222)	(3 309)
Private Sector with Public Guarantee	21	30	46	48	76	72	69	62	1 463	1 718	2 001	2 935	2 674
Private Sector	670	799	990	1 570	2 736	4 693	8 138	8 658	6 742	6 362	5 135	3 435	2 466
Banks and Financial Institutions	(38)	(9)	(15)	(275)	(768)	(2 169)	(4 690)	(4 971)	(3 394)	(3 369)	(2 691)	(1 296)	(502)
Corporates and Private Debtors[1]	(632)	(790)	(975)	(1 295)	(1 968)	(2 524)	(3 448)	(3 790)	(3 441)	(3 065)	(2 579)	(2 275)	(2 091)

III. Short-term external debt	**587**	**446**	**691**	**741**	**977**	**1 671**	**2 989**	**3 338**	**2 599**	**1 914**	**1 794**	**1 687**	**2 017**
Public Sector	471	287	397	356	292	343	1 050	1 503	1 705	1 742	1 564	1 384	1 655
Public Financial Sector	285	97	75	158	9	4	4	471	568	594	444	117	252
Banco del Estado	(152)	(97)	(70)	(153)	(9)	(4)	(4)	(271)	(268)	(114)	(119)	(117)	(27)
Central Bank	(113)	(0)	(5)	(5)	(0)	(0)	(0)	(200)	(300)	(480)	(325)	(0)	(225)
Public non-financial Sector	186	190	322	198	283	339	1 046	1 032	785	736	773	794	801
Treasury	(0)	(0)	(0)	(0)	(0)	(0)	(0)	(24)	(24)	(0)	(0)	(0)	(0)
Others	(166)	(190)	(322)	(198)	(283)	(339)	(1 046)	(1 008)	(761)	(736)	(773)	(794)	(801)
Private Sector with Public Guarantee	0	0	0	0	0	0	0	0	352	412	347	473	602
Private Sector	116	159	294	385	685	1 328	1 939	1 835	894	172	230	303	362
Banks and Financial Institutions	(116)	(159)	(294)	(385)	(685)	(1 328)	(1 939)	(1 732)	(801)	(100)	(95)	(167)	(235)
Corporate and Private Debtors[1]	(0)	(0)	(0)	(0)	(0)	(0)	(0)	(103)	(93)	(72)	(135)	(136)	(127)
IV. Central bank with IMF	**434**	**513**	**412**	**347**	**179**	**123**	**49**	**6**	**606**	**782**	**1 085**	**1 328**	**1 452**

* Excludes external debt repayable in local currency. Includes reductions owing to external debt conversion (chapters XVIII, XIX and others).

1. Excludes a portion of short-term credits to non-banks for operation in foreign trade.

Source: *Chilean External Debt 1987*, Central Bank of Chile, February 1989.

Table 1.10. CHILE – EXTERNAL DEBT AND PRINCIPAL RATIOS

Millions of US$

	1975	1980	1982	1983	1984	1985	1986	1987
External debt								
Total external debt (EDT)	4 761.6	12 081.3	17 314.7	18 096.3	19 844.0	20 313.0	20 899.7	21 424.5
Long-Term Debt	4 374.3	9 398.5	13 970.4	14 891.1	17 150.8	17 556.9	17 994.5	18 051.9
Public & Publicly Guaranteed	3 733.3	4 705.2	5 244.4	6 766.1	10 723.8	12 825.9	14 559.5	15 585.9
Official Creditors	2 098.2	1 367.1	1 185.3	1 453.4	1 611.7	2 051.6	2 929.5	3 903.8
Private Creditors	1 635.2	3 338.1	4 059.1	5 312.7	9 112.1	10 774.3	11 630.1	11 682.0
Suppliers	584.1	438.0	313.7	373.7	402.4	349.6	378.8	513.0
Financial Markets	540.5	2 639.3	3 564.1	4 801.5	8 507.4	10 249.6	11 115.4	11 076.2
Private Non-guaranteed	641.0	4 693.3	8 726.0	8 125.0	6 427.0	4 731.0	3 435.0	2 466.0
Use of IMF Credit	387.3	122.8	6.3	606.2	779.3	1 088.1	1 331.1	1 464.6
Short-Term Debt	0.0	2 560.0	3 338.0	2 599.0	1 914.0	1 668.0	1 574.0	1 908.0
Principal ratios								
Total External Debt								
EDT/XGS (%)	258.5	192.5	335.9	374.6	412.2	435.1	390.7	330.2
EDT/GNP (%)	68.7	45.3	77.1	100.2	115.1	144.1	140.0	125.2
RES/EDT (%)	5.0	34.2	15.0	14.5	14.0	14.5	14.1	15.1
RES/MGS (months)	1.2	5.9	4.1	5.2	4.8	5.8	5.4	5.2
Public & Publicly Guaranteed Debt								
DOD/XGS (%)	202.7	75.0	101.8	140.1	222.8	274.7	272.2	240.2
DOD/GNP (%)	53.8	17.7	23.3	37.5	62.2	91.0	97.5	91.1
TDS/XGS (%)	27.2	21.9	19.8	18.1	25.7	26.3	28.5	20.9
TDS/GNP (%)	7.2	5.2	4.5	4.8	7.2	8.7	10.2	7.9
INT/XGS (%)	8.5	7.7	10.6	11.4	19.2	21.3	23.1	17.6
INT/GNP (%)	2.3	1.8	2.4	3.1	5.4	7.1	8.3	6.7
RES/DOD (%)	6.4	87.7	49.5	38.7	25.9	23.0	20.3	20.8

Notes: EDT : Total External Debt
XGS : Exports of Goods and Services
GNP : Gross National Product
TSD : Total Debt Services
RES : International Reserves
MGS : Imports of Goods and Services
DOD : Debt Outstanding and Disbursed
INT : Interest Payments

Source: *World Bank.*

while public and publicly-guaranteed debt has risen. Between 1984 and 1987, outstanding debt to commercial banks was reduced, but this was offset by more debt to multilateral institutions. Approximately four-fifths of Chile's debt is based on variable rates; thus, to limit exposure to international interest rates, in late 1987 the Central Bank of Chile began to hedge between $1-2 billion of its obligations against interest rate fluctuations.

The observed reduction of debt-service payments is due to falling interest rates, Chile's innovative debt management policies, and refinancing that has resulted in lower amortization payments. Hence, if rescheduled amortization had been included in the debt-service ratio, the ratio would have been much worse in 1987.

Chile's projected debt-service obligations are shown in Table 1.11. While the debt-service obligation of the Chilean private sector (projected non-guaranteed) is expected to decline after 1989, the public sector's is expected to increase. Chile's public sector debt-servicing obligations to private creditors, more or less constant until 1990, will jump dramatically in 1991 – from $1 285 million to $2 037 million. This increased debt servicing from 1991 to 1995 springs from prior rescheduling agreements (Chapter 2). These projections may be affected, of course, by further reschedulings, changes in interest rates, innovative debt management policies or debt-relief measures.

Mexico

Mexico's total external debt also increased beginning in 1975. It soared from $15 608 million in 1975 to $109 492 million in 1987 (see Table 1.12). The major cause has been long-term debt, which grew from $15 608 million in 1975 to $98 529 million in 1987; and the lion's share of this debt has been the public and publicly-guaranteed component, namely $11 414 million in 1975 and $84 381 million in 1987. The contribution of official and private creditors to this debt varied over this period. In 1975, with meagre oil revenues, official creditors gave 20 per cent. By 1980 the contribution of official creditors had declined to 13.2 per cent. This fall resulted from an increase in Mexico's proven oil reserves, higher oil prices, a rapid growth of development expenditures in 1977 because of optimistic oil revenue projections and the willingness of commercial banks to lend to Mexico. The contribution of official creditors reached a low of 10 per cent in 1983 and 1984 but rose after banks pulled back their lending; in 1987, the contribution of official creditors to Mexico's outstanding long-term public and publicly-guaranteed debt had increased to 18.9 per cent.

Although Mexico's external financing grew rapidly, gross public investment as a percentage of GDP public investment suffered during the period 1970-1974 and is currently below its 1970-1974 average (see Table 1.13). Instead Mexican debt has had its mirror image in capital flight (see Table 1.14), a direct result of domestic macro-economic policies.

Heavy external borrowing is vividly reflected in a variety of debt ratios (see Table 1.12). Total external debt to exports of goods and services, while falling from 245.25 in 1975 to 233.3 per cent in 1980 (because of sharply higher oil revenues) flew to 311.2 per cent in 1982 and to 426.7 per cent in 1986, with the latter deterioration reflecting the collapse of the oil market; in 1987, this ratio stood at 367.9 per cent. Total external debt to GNP increased almost continuously from 17.2 per cent in 1975 to 82.5 per cent in 1986 before falling to 78.6 per cent in 1987, while the debt-service ratio increased from 24.9 per cent in 1975 to 40 per cent in 1983, before falling to 32.6 per cent in 1987.

The recent decline in Mexico's debt-service ratio reflects cuts in interest rates and especiallly debt restructuring (see Chapter 4); debt management schemes have also

Table 1.11. CHILE – DEBT SERVICES PROJECTIONS

US$ millions

	1991	1992	1993	1994	1995	1996	1997
Projected Public Debt Service	2 826	2 905	2 914	2 547	2 398	2 140	1 945
Principal	1 439	1 475	1 792	1 574	1 560	1 437	1 365
Interest	1 387	1 429	1 122	973	838	703	581
Official Creditors	789	799	747	695	667	605	560
Principal	441	475	455	437	433	416	405
Interest	348	324	292	258	224	189	155
Private Creditors	2 037	2 106	2 167	1 852	1 741	1 535	1 387
Principal	998	1 000	1 337	1 136	1 127	1 021	960
Interest	1 039	1 106	831	715	614	514	426
Projected Non-guaranteed Debt Service	342	319	295	262	245	227	214
Principal	186	178	169	150	145	140	138
Interest	157	141	126	112	100	87	76
Projected Total Long-Term Debt Service	3 168	3 224	3 210	2 809	2 643	2 367	2 160
Principal	1 624	1 653	1 961	1 724	1 706	1 577	1 503
Interest	1 680	1 571	1 249	1 086	937	791	657

Source: *World Debt Tables,* World Bank, Vol. II, 1988-89 Editions.

Table 1.12. MEXICO - EXTERNAL DEBT AND PRINCIPAL RATIOS

US$ million

	1975	1980	1982	1983	1984	1985	1986	1987
External debt								
Total external debt (EDT)	15 608.5	57 450.3	86 110.5	93 056.6	94 907.6	96 875.3	101 053.7	109 492.2
Long-Term Debt	15 608.5	41 287.3	59 742.2	81 657.3	86 107.7	88 455.9	91 093.5	96 529.2
Public & publicly guaranteed	11 413.7	33 987.3	51 842.2	66 857.3	89 811.7	72 710.9	75 990.5	84 381.2
Official Creditors	2 293.3	4 480.5	6 958.2	6 712.5	6 996.1	8 873.0	11 773.3	15 939.2
Private Creditors	9 120.4	29 506.8	44 684.0	60 144.8	62 815.6	63 837.9	64 217.2	68 441.9
Suppliers	513.5	256.9	182.4	366.6	209.1	228.7	258.2	263.0
Financial Markets	8 606.9	29 249.9	44 501.6	59 778.2	62 606.5	63 609.2	63 959.0	68 179.0
Private Non-guaranteed	4 194.8	7 300.0	8 100.0	14 800.0	16 296.0	15 746.0	15 103.0	14 148.0
Use of IMF credit	0.0	0.0	221.3	1 260.3	2 359.9	2 969.4	4 060.1	5 163.0
Short-Term Debt	0.0	16 163.0	26 147.0	10 139.0	6 440.0	5 450.0	5 900.0	5 800.0
Principal ratios								
Total External Debt								
EDT/XGS (%)	245.2	233.3	311.2	325.2	292.3	325.7	426.7	367.9
EDT/GNP (%)	17.2	30.4	52.6	66.4	57.2	54.9	82.5	78.6
RES/EDT (%)	12.2	7.3	2.1	5.2	8.4	5.9	6.6	12.5
RES/MGS (months)	2.2	1.5	0.6	2.4	3.4	2.3	3.1	6.2
Public and Publicly Guaranteed Debt								
DOD/XGS (%)	179.3	138.0	186.6	233.7	215.0	244.5	320.9	283.5
DOD/GNP (%)	12.5	18.0	31.5	47.7	42.1	41.2	62.0	60.6
TDS/XGS (%)	24.9	32.1	34.1	40.0	34.8	35.7	37.3	32.6
TDS/GNP (%)	1.7	4.2	5.8	8.2	6.8	6.0	7.2	7.0
INT/XGS (%)	13.0	15.8	22.3	23.1	22.8	25.3	26.4	21.6
INT/GNP (%)	0.9	2.1	3.8	4.7	4.5	4.3	5.1	4.6
RES/DOD (%)	16.6	12.3	3.4	7.2	11.5	7.8	8.8	16.2

Notes: EDT : Total External Debt
XGS : Exports of Goods and Services
GNP : Gross National Product
TSD : Total Debt Services
RES : International Reserves
MGS : Imports of Goods and Services
DOD : Debt Outstanding and Disbursed
INT : Interest Payments

Source: *World Bank.*

Table 1.13. GROSS INVESTMENT
% of GDP

	Total	Public	Private
1970-1974	19.2	6.5	12.8
1975-1979	21.3	8.9	12.4
1980-1984	21.5	9.5	12.0
1985	16.9	6.0	10.9
1986	15.5	5.2	10.3
1987	15.3	5.1	10.2

Banco de Mexico and for 1985-1987, Hacienda Mexico: Economic and Financial Statistics, November 1987.
Source: Dornbusch, 1988.

contributed. Mexico's projected debt-service obligations are shown in Table 1.15. While those of the private sector are expected to decline without interruption, the public sector's are projected to increase sharply in 1991 before falling. Again these estimates could be affected by further reschedulings, changes in interest rates, innovative debt management schemes or debt relief measures.

Table 1.14. DEBT AND CAPITAL FLIGHT (1976-1985)
$ billions

Capital flight	
1976-1982	36.0
1983-1985	17.0
Total	53.0
Mexican deposits abroad	
1985	15.3
Debt without capital flight	
Actual Debt	97
Without Capital Flight (including savings in interest)	12

Source: *World Financial Markets,* Morgan Guaranty Trust, 1987, No. II.

Table 1.15. MEXICO – DEBT SERVICES PROJECTIONS

US$ millions

	1991	1992	1993	1994	1995	1996	1997
Projected Public Debt Service	14 926	11 289	10 420	9 483	8 250	9 184	7 654
Principal	8 378	6 389	4 980	4 479	3 585	4 882	3 740
Interest	6 548	5 880	5 440	5 004	4 664	4 302	3 914
Official Creditors	3 314	3 442	3 112	2 818	2 528	2 166	1 461
Principal	1 966	2 230	2 083	1 966	1 846	1 646	1 078
Interest	1 348	1 213	1 029	862	683	519	383
Private Creditors	11 611	7 826	7 308	6 665	6 722	7 018	6 193
Principal	6 412	3 159	2 897	2 514	1 741	3 235	2 662
Interest	5 200	4 667	4 411	4 151	3 982	3 783	3 531
Projected Non-Guaranteed Debt Service	2 290	1 120	1 507	567	559	3 143	0
Principal	1 759	676	1 140	260	274	3 015	0
Interest	531	444	367	307	286	128	0
Projected Total Long-Term Debt Service	17 215	12 389	11 927	10 060	8 809	12 327	7 654
Principal	10 137	6 065	6 120	4 739	3 859	7 897	3 740
Interest	7 079	6 324	5 807	5 311	4 949	4 430	3 914

Source: *World Debt Tables,* World Bank, Vol. II, 1988-89 Editions.

NOTES

1. For a discussion of growth prospectives of Third World Countries, see *World Economic Outlook,* IMF, April 1988.
2. See IMF, *World Economic Outlook,* April 1989.
3. See Krugman, P.R., "Financing vs. Forgiving: A Debt Overhang", First InterAmerican Seminar on Economics, Mexico City, March 17-19, 1988.
4. For more information, available sources are: the *World Debt Tables* and *World Development Report* of the World Bank, *World Economic Outlook* and the *Annual Report* of the IMF, and the *Annual Report* of the BIS.
5. This group consists of fifteen countries outlined in the Baker plan – Argentina, Bolivia, Brazil, Chile, Colombia, Côte d'Ivoire, Ecuador, Mexico, Morocco, Nigeria, Peru, Philippines, Uruguay, Venezuela, and Yugoslavia.
6. Proposal put forward by the U.S. Secretary of the Treasury, James Baker III, before the joint Annual Meetings of the IMF and the World Bank, Seoul, Korea, October 8, 1985.
7. For a statistical survey of commercial banks and their LDC debt, consult Askari, H. and Papalexopoulou, A., "Third World Debt: The Contributions of Financial Innovation to the Financing of Development", OECD (Development Centre) Working Paper, February 1989.
8. See *World Economic Outlook,* IMF, April 1988, p. 117.
9. Speech by Mr. M. Camdessus, as reported in the *IMF Survey,* May 16, 1988.
10. For a balanced analysis, see Anne O. Krueger, "Resolving the Debt Crisis and Restoring Developing Countries' Creditworthiness", IMF Seminar, June 2, 1988.
11. It is partly for this reason that the approach to ameliorating the debt situation has been on a case-by-case basis.
12. See *Annual Report 1983,* IMF.
13. See *Annual Report 1981,* IMF.
14. For a discussion of the impact of the OECD recession, see *Annual Report* of the IMF, 1982-1986.
15. For a discussion of protectionism, see Jagdish Bhagwati, *Protectionism,* M.I.T. Press, 1988.
16. See *Annual Report 1983,* IMF.
17. Average annual percentage euro-dollar interest rates were 5.6 (1976), 6.0 (1977), 8.7 (1978), 12.0 (1979), 14.4 (1980), 16.5 (1981), 13.1 (1982).
18. See *External Debt of Developing Countries,* OECD, Paris, 1983.
19. While financial and economic conditions for debtor countries were deteriorating, commercial banks "appeared" to be profiting. For example, irrespective of the relative contribution of income from loans to the non-oil developing countries, overall contribution of international earnings to total income of banks in the United States increased dramatically after 1979, reaching 52.2 per cent of total earnings in 1981 (Salomon Brothers inc., Bank Securities Department, 1984). The more lucrative markets were obviously away from home, and banks did not hesitate to follow them, albeit uncautiously, judging by the rapid expansion of loans.

20. However, current account deficits could indicate profitable investment opportunities.
21. Stanley Fischer, "Economic Growth and Economic Policy", *Symposium on Growth-Oriented Adjustment,* World Bank and the International Monetary Fund, Washington, D.C., 25-27 February 1987, pp. 31-32 and Arnold Harberger, "Economic Policy and Economic Growth", in A.C. Harberger (ed), *World Economic Growth,* Institute for Contemporary Studies, San Francisco, 1984.
22. For instance, in the cases of Brazil and Argentina.
23. For an early reference to this difficulty, see Rudiger Dornbusch, "Policy and Performance Links between LDC Debtors and Individual Nations", *Brookings Papers on Economic Activity,* No. 2, 1985. For an excellent and detailed discussion see Helmut Reisen, *Public Developing Country Debt, External Competitiveness, and Required Fiscal Discipline,* Princeton Studies in International Finance, No. 161, September 1989.
24. See Reisen, 1989 op. cit. and Helmut Reisen and Axel van Trotsenburg, *Developing Country Debt: The Budgetary and Transfer Problem.* OECD Development Centre Studies, 1988.
25. For practical discussions of debt-equity swaps, see "Guide to Debt Equity Swaps", *The Economist,* September 1987.
26. Clearly the principal could be collateralised by any high quality paper, and not necessarily that of the U.S. or any other government.
27. See Telljohann, Kenneth and Richard Buckholz, *The Mexican Bonds Exchange Offer,* Salomon Brothers, January 1988.
28. The U.S. Congressional Research Service has compiled a most impressive compendium of such plans. Suggestions have come from many sources – heads of state, ministers, bankers, businessmen, academics and others. The plans vary: some focus on existing debt, others consider new money flows; some are country-specific, while others benefit all Third World debtors; some call for partial debt relief, and others call for total; some involve third party guarantees, others do not; some involve swaps and benefit from selling debt at a discount, others do not; some recommend tying of debt-servicing to performance, while others go as far as suggesting a restructuring of the world economy. The major problems with most, if not all, such plans is that they do not apportion sacrifices evenly, they are not put forth by all concerned parties and as a result, they do not attract universal agreement and commitment. See Patricia Wertman, "The International Debt Problem: Options For Solution", Library of Congress, October 1984.
29. In light of this, a survey of all major banks in creditor countries was conducted. The results are summarised in Askari and Papalexopoulou, *op. cit.*
30. The Brady Plan was suggested by Secretary Brady to the Brookings Institution and the Bretton Woods Committee Conference on Third World Debt on March 10, 1989. This proposal was made after the draft of this study was completed. There is a brief discussion of the Brady Plan here, followed by further considerations in Chapters 3 and 4.
31. For a discussion of future projects, see Chapter 4.
32. For a discussion of recent economic performance of the problem debtors see *World Economic Outlook,* IMF, April 1988.
33. See *Innovations in International Banking,* BIS, April 1986.
34. See "Consultative paper: proposals for international convergence of capital measurement and capital standards", Committee on Banking Regulations and Supervisory Practices, BIS, December, 1987. This proposal was endorsed by Central Bank governors in July 1988. The agreed standard ratio of capital to risk assets is 8 per cent; with half of the capital to consist of equity and disclosed reserves as core capital.
35. For a more detailed discussion see Askari and Papalexopoulou, *op. cit.* Appendix II.
36. These same facts can be alternatively interpreted – banks in countries whose currencies have appreciated have implicitly been "forced" to recognise losses due to the dollar's depreciation.

37. For a detailed discussion of accounting and tax regulations, see Peat Marwick, *Bank Tax Conference*, 1988.
38. See Paul R. Krugman, "Market-based Debt-Reduction Schemes", NBER Working Paper Series No. 2587, May 1988.
39. Unfortunately, the trade surplus of many developing countries has been caused by import compression, as opposed to export expansion. For the period 1981-1985, the almost $50 billion in trade balance improvement for the Baker countries was due to a $56 billion reduction in imports, and their exports in 1985 were $7 billion lower that in 1981. (See Shafiqul Islam, "Breaking the International Debt Deadlock", Council on Foreign Relations, Critical Issues 1988:2, p. 14.)
40. This discussion of flight capital is largely based on *Capital Flight and Third World Debt,* Donald R. Lessard and John Williamson (editors), Institute for International Economics, Washington, D.C., 1987.
41. Such policies are difficult to implement if only because the people who have contributed to capital outflows are those likely to be in power.
42. See Krugman for a lucid discussion of this point.
43. Various newspaper reports quoting investment bankers indicate that transactions on the secondary market for Third World debt can be expected to be around $15 billion in 1988. See *WSJ,* May 17, 1988.
44. See "Buy-backs and the Market Valuation of External Debt", IMF working paper, September 1987.
45. See Krugman, 1988.
46. Although this specific issue has not been addressed, creditor countries have often recognised the necessity of debt forgiveness for the poorest countries. Most recently, on June 8, 1988, President Mitterand of France suggested that the Group of Seven should make substantial concessions on repayment of principal and interest to the heavily indebted poorer developing countries. He indicated that France would in any case unilaterally forgive (write off) one-third of the debt owed by twenty poor countries – with *per capita* income of less than $500, debt exceeding 30 per cent of GDP and with a record of debt management approved by The Paris Club. This is a start in the right direction.
47. See Corbo, 1985.

Chapter 2

DEBT MANAGEMENT IN CHILE

Introduction

As mentioned in Chapter 1, the accumulation of external debt in Chile was rather unique in one important respect: it was largely due to the private sector. By late 1981, the gross debt of the public sector stood at $5.4 billion and net international reserves were $3.8 billion, for a net external debt of $1.6 billion; while the private sector's gross debt was $10.1 billion, net international reserves were –$1.1 billion, for a net external debt of $11.2 billion[1]. As a result, by late 1981 net private sector external debt constituted around 87 per cent of total external debt.

The reasons for this are rooted in macro-economic policies. Essentially, the Chilean public sector did not face the same budgetary crunch as did other problem debtor countries. In fact, between 1975 and 1981, net external public debt shrank from $4.2 billion to $1.6 billion; while gross debt grew, external borrowing was used to increase international reserves. This unusual performance by a major debtor was spurred by the strong fiscal reform begun under the military government in 1974 which turned a large budget deficit into consistent surplus by 1976. On the other hand, the surge in the private sector's net external debt from $2.4 billion by late 1978 to $11.2 billion by late 1981 was used to finance private spending and resulted in unsustainable levels of current account deficits. During this period 1979-1981, domestic credit demand expanded while the government pursued a fixed exchange rate policy (to slow inflation, resulting in relatively low-cost dollar loans), and in mid 1979 the government eliminated restrictions on external borrowing. The consequence was massive external borrowing by the private sector, mostly accomplished with Chilean commercial banks acting as intermediaries. These developments produced another unique characteristic of the accumulation of Chilean debt: Chile, unlike other Latin American debtors, did not experience much capital flight. Larrain (1986), quoting Avellano and Ramos (1987), states that during 1975-1981, there was unregistered captial inflow and during 1982-1983, capital flight was only $1 billion, accounting for about 5 per cent of Chile's external debt.

This trend changed after the onset of the debt crisis in 1982. Chile's current account deficit declined from $4.8 billion in 1981 to $2.4 billion in 1982. This reversal was produced through an even bigger turn-around in the trade account, from a deficit of $3.2 billion in 1981 to a slight surplus in 1982; the trade surplus widened further in 1983 because of an uninterrupted fall in imports. Expansionary policies in 1984 temporarily reversed this development, but in early 1985 Chile began a more stable policy, focusing on a reduction in the current account deficit.

From 1982 through 1988, a major structural change occurred in Chile's external debt. At the end of 1981, on the brink of the crisis, Chile's external indebtedness largely belonged to the private sector (about 87 per cent of net external debt and 65 per cent of its gross external debt). This situation was reversed in ensuing years. By the end of 1988, this sector's net external debt obligations were barely over 30 per cent (and under 30 per cent of gross external debt). Here we will give a summary of the policies Chile used.

The turn-around in private-public external debt obligations took place because of several developments. First, in January 1983, a financial crisis occurred for some domestic financial institutions. Two banks and a finance company had to be liquidated, and the country's two largest private commercial banks (with 35-40 per cent of the outstanding credit to the private sector) faced severe liquidity problems. All had accumulated substantial external debts. With liquidation and restructuring, their obligations were passed on to the Chilean public sector. Specifically, the government took over some of these obligations and, more importantly, it guaranteed the debt of the financial sector as it became due[2]. The commercial banks had pressured the government of Chile to do this. In retrospect, the Minister of Finance should not have capitulated so easily. Commercial banks, however, argued that it was vital for external confidence in the Chilean economy and to keep creditors engaged. In any case, by late 1988, about 90 per cent of Chile's external debt was public or publicly guaranteed. Through a variety of policies – preferential exchange rates, interest rate subsidies, purchase of bad loans – the government absorbed a large proportion of the private sector's accumulated external debt (Larrain 1986). Larrain (1988*b*) estimates the cost of these programmes at $6 billion. The government of Chile was able to accomplish this feat because of its own sound fiscal condition in 1981. However, this responsibility has clearly worsened the government's own finances.

A second contributing factor to the structural change in public-private debt has been the proportionally higher use of debt reduction schemes by the private sector. Also, after the crisis, private sector access to new external financing had to be guaranteed by the public sector. Finally, the government had to borrow to finance interest payments on external debt.

The focus of this chapter is an analysis of Chile's debt management policies since 1982. Their major components have been:

- rescheduling;
- formal or official debt reduction schemes;
- informal debt reduction schemes;
- hedging operations and other policies.

Rescheduling

Beginning in 1983, Chile was active in renegotiating its external debt. Its attitude has been one of co-operation with its creditors. Chile has honoured all its external obligations – an international framework of debt negotiations set up by major creditors, creditor steering committees, loan procedures, agreements with IMF and World Bank, etc.[3] Chile has not adopted unilateral moves but instead has relied on multi-year rescheduling agreements to extend repayment of principal, repricing of interest rate margins on new and existing credits and obtaining new money to meet its financing requirements. Chile's handling of reschedulings has been "...direct, consistent, expeditious, and serious, avoiding delays and other deficiencies observed elsewhere" (Garces, 1988). Swift resolution has been more important to Chile than a slight benefit in interest rate spreads; for other Latin debtors, usually the opposite has been true. Chilean authorities have also worked closely with the World Bank and the IMF, following their programmes for rescheduling agreements and concurring with their conditionalities.

The following major benefits to Chile's debt renegotiation can be listed:

i) for commercial debt, repayment and grace periods have been lengthened at each renegotiation;
ii) rescheduling has also applied to loans since 1983;
iii) the interest rate spreads over LIBOR or prime have declined dramatically from 2.25 per cent to 13/16 per cent for pre-1982 credits and to 7/8 per cent to all post-1982 credits;
iv) flat one-time rescheduling and new money fees, which had been 1.25 per cent of the face value of the rescheduled amount in 1983, were reduced to 0.625 per cent, to 0.5 per cent and the to 0 in 1987 (no new money has been requested from commercial banks since 1986);
v) the frequency of interest payments has been lengthened – from quarterly to semi-annually in 1985 and to annually in 1987; the one-time savings that resulted were $170 million in 1985 and $480 in 1988 (Larrain, 1988*b*); and
vi) lower costs for co-financing loans.

Debt renegotiation and rescheduling are one aspect of Chile's debt reduction effort. Although other debtors have used similar methods, Chile stands out because of its interest in rapid negotiations and its use of a regulatory framework within official debt reduction schemes. In this area, Chile has been a leader.

Formal Debt Reduction Schemes

A major foundation for formal debt reduction schemes is a sizeable secondary market discount for a country's debt. After the onset of the debt crisis, a small secondary market for some Third World debt developed, with all major debtor paper selling at a discount ($2 billion in 1985, $5 billion in 1986, $10 billion in 1987). On the supply side, creditors with small exposure wanted to sell some of their loans to avoid rescheduling and lending new money. As for demand, debtor countries like Chile that were paying interest on the full face value of the paper became attracted to buying back their own paper at a discount. This market was initially small and even today it has remained a small secondary market compared to the outstanding commercial debt of major debtors. In 1988, the total volume of transactions in the secondary market was estimated as $17-$20 billion, but its growth has been quite fast since 1985. Typical market discounts are shown in Table 2.1.

The size of the secondary market is restricted by many factors. Unfavourable accounting and tax treatment for banks in creditor countries and restrictive clauses in syndicated loan agreements are foremost – negative pledges, sharing provisions, mandatory repayments, *pari passu,* new money terms, waiver modifications and cross-default clauses all create obstacles in the secondary market. The negative pledge clause eliminates discrimination among creditors through selective pledging of assets. The cross-default clause and the negative pledge ensure that at a time of a debt-servicing crisis all creditors have the same rights. Mandatory repayment stipulates that if a debtor prepays any rescheduled debt, it has to prepay all of its rescheduled debt on a *pro rata* basis. These three provisions alone would not allow debtors to buy their own loans unless they obtained exceptions from their creditors. Similarly, debt-equity swaps require amendments or waivers based on the acceptance that such swaps are tantamount to prepayment. Thus an amendment is required to

Table 2.1. SECONDARY MARKET PRICES ON SELECTED EXTERNAL DEBT

Country	12/12/86	19/12/86	26/12/86	02/01/87	09/01/87	16/01/87	23/01/87	30/01/87	06/02/87	13/02/87	20/02/87	27/02/87	06/03/87	13/03/87	20/03/87
Argentina	65-66	65-66	65-66	65-66	65-66	65-66	65-66	65-66	65-66	65-66	65-66	65-66	64-65	64-65	64
Brazil	75-77	75-77	75-77	75-77	75-77	74.5-76.5	75-76	75-76	74.5-75.5	74-75	–	66-67	65-67	65-67	65-67
Chile	68-69	68-69	68-69	68-69	68-69	68.5-69.5	68-70	69-70	69-70	69-70	69-70	69-70	69-70	69-70	69-70
Mexico	55-56	55-56	55-56	55-56	55.5-56.5	56-57	56-57	56.5-57.5	57-58	57.5-58.5	58-59	57.5-58.5	57.5-58.5	57.5-58.5	58-60
Philippines							74-75			72.5-74.5	72.5-74.5	72-74		72-73.5	72-73.5
Venezuela	73-74	74-75	74-75	74-75	74-75	74-75	74-75	74-75	74-75	73.75-74.5	73.75-74.5	73-74	73.5-74.5	73.5-74.5	73-74

Country	27/03/87	03/04/87	10/04/87	17/04/87	24/04/87	30/04/87	08/05/87	15/05/87	22/05/87	29/05/87	05/06/87	12/06/87	19/06/87	26/06/87	03/07/87
Argentina	64	60-62	60-62	60-62	59-60	59-60	58.5-60.5	59.5-60.5	59.5-60.5	58-59	58-59	52-53	52-53	51-52	48-49
Brazil	65-67	63-65	63-65	63-65	63-65	63-65	63-65	64-65	64-65	63.5-64.5	63-64	62-63	61-62	60-61	60.61
Chile	69-70	69-70	69-70	69-70	70-71	70-71	70-71	70-71	70-71	70-71	70-71	69-70	69-69.5	68-69	68-69
Mexico	58-60	59-60	59-60	59-60	58.5-59.5	58.5-59.5	58.5-59.5	58.5-59.5	58.5-59.5	58-59	57.5-58.5	57-58	56.25-57.75	56-57	55.5-56.5
Philippines	72-73.5	72	72	72	72	72-72.5	72-72.5	72-72.5	72-72.5	70.5-71	70.5-71	70.5-71	69-70.5	69-70.5	68-69
Venezuela	73-74	73	73	73	73	73	73	73-74	73-74	73-74	72-73	70-71	70.5-71	70.5-71	70-71

Country	10/07/87	17/07/87	24/07/87	31/07/87	07/08/87	14/08/87	21/08/87	28/08/87	04/09/87	11/09/87	18/09/87	25/09/87	02/10/87	09/10/87	16/10/87
Argentina	48-49	48-49	48-49	47-48	46-47	45-46	42-44	41-43	41-42	38-39	37-38	37-38	36-37	35-36	35-36
Brazil	59-60	57-58	55-56	52-53	51-52	50-51	45-48	45-48	42-44	40-42	40-42	40-42	40-41	30-40	39-41
Chile	67-69	67-69	66-68	66-67	65-66	64-65	62-63	60-62	59-61	57-59	56-57	54-55	53-54	52-53	51-52
Ecuador								37.5-38.5	38-39	38-39	38-39	37-39	36-38	36-38	35-38
Mexico	53-54	53.5-54.5	53.5-54.5	53-54	52-53	50-51	49-50	48.5-49.5	48.5-49.5	48-49	48-49	48-48.5	47-48	47-48	48.5-49.5
Philippines	68-69	68-69	68-69	68-69	68-69	68-69	67.68	65-67	64-66	64-66	61-63	60-61	59-60	54-55	52-53
Poland					41-42	41-42	41-42	41-42	41-42	41-42	41-42	41-42	41-42	41-42	41-42
Venezuela	68-70	67-69	66-68	66-67	65-66	64-65	62.63	58.60	55-56	55-56	51.5-53	52-53	51-52	49-51	49-51

Country	23/10/87	30/10/87	06/11/87	13/11/87	20/11/87	30/11/87	04/12/87	11/12/87	18/12/87	31/12/87	08/01/88	15/01/88	22/01/88	29/01/88	05/02/88
Argentina	37-38	36-37	36-37	37.5-38.5	38-39	37-39	37-38	35-37	28-30	28-33	28-33	28-33	28-31	27-29	26-28
Brazil	40-41	41-43	43-46	49.5-50.5	48-49	47-49	47-48	47-48	46-47	46-47	46-47	46-47	46-47	46-46.5	46-46.5
Chile	52-53	52-53	53-54	54-56	59-60	60-62	61-62	61-62	62-63	60-61	61-62	61-62	60-61	61-63	60-62
Ecuador	35-39	33-34	33-35	34-36	35-37	37-39	37-39	37-39	36.5-37.5	36-37	36-37	36-37	35-36	35-36	35-36
Honduras										28-30	28-30	28-30	28-30	26-28	25-27
Mexico	52-53	51-52	53-54	52-53	52-53	53-54	53-54	53-54	50.5-51	50.5-51.5	49-51.5	49-51.5	48-49	46-47.5	47-48
Philippines	53-54	50-51	50-51	51-52	51-52.5	51.5-52.5	52-53	52-53	52-53	50-51	50-51	50-51	50-51	50-51	50-51
Poland	41-42	41-42	41-42	41-42	41-42	41-42	41-42	41-42	41-42	41-42	41-42	41-42	41-42	41-42	41-42
Venezuela	50-51	50-52	51-53	51-53	60-61	59-61	61-62	59-61	58-59	57-58	54-55	55-56	56-57	55-57	54-55

	12/02/88	19/02/88	26/02/88	04/03/88	11/03/88	18/03/88	25/03/88	31/03/88	08/04/88	15/04/88	22/04/88	29/04/88	06/05/88	15/05/88	31/05/88
Argentina	27-29	27-28	27-28	27-28	27-28	27-28	28-29	28-29	28-29	28-29	28-29	28	28	28	28
Brazil	46-46.5	46-47	46-47	46-47	46.5-47.5	47.5-48.5	50-51	50-51	50-51	51-52	52-53.5	53-53.5	54-54.5	56-56.375	54.5-54.75
Chile	60-61.5	60-61	60-61	59.5-60.5	60-61	59-60	59-60	59-60	59-60	60	61	60-61	60-61	61-62	61-62
Ecuador	35-36	35-36	35	33-35	32-33	32-33	32-33	32-33	30-32	30-31	29	28-29	27-28	25	25
Honduras	25-27	26-28	26-28	25-27	25-26	24-25	24-25	24-25	24-25	24-25	24-25	24-25	24-25	24-25	24-25
Mexico	48-49	48-49	49	47-48	48-49	48.5-49.5	51-52	51-52	50.5-51.5	51.5-52	52-52.5	52.5-53	53-53.5	54.5	53.75-54
Philippines	50-51	50-51	50-51	50-51	51-51.5	51-51.5	51-51.5	51-51.5	52-52.5	52-53	53-54	54-54.5	55-56	55	55
Poland	42-43	42-43	42-43	42.5-43.5	43-44	43-44	43-44	43-44	43-44	43-44	43-44	44	43-44	43-44	43-44
Venezuela	54-55	54-55	54	53-54	53-54	53-54	54	54	54-55	54-55	54-55.5	55-55.5	555-56	57-57.5	57

	03/06/88	10/06/88	17/06/88	24/06/88	01/07/88	08/07/88	15/07/88	22/07/88	29/07/88
Argentina	27	26	25	24.5	24	25	25.5	26-26.5	26-26.5
Brazil	53-53.25	52.5	51.5-52	51	51.5	53	52.5	52.5	51.5
Chile	60-61	61	61	61.5	61.25	62	61.5	61-61.5	60.75-61.25
Ecuador	25	25	25	25	25	25	26	26.5	27
Honduras	24-25	24-25	24-25	24-25	24-25	24-25	24-25	24-25	24-25
Mexico	53	51.5	51	50	51	51.75	51.5	51.5	50.5
Philippines	54	52	53	54	54	54	54	54	54
Poland	43	43	42	43	41.5	41.5	41.5	41	40
Venezuela	56.5	56.5	56	56	55.5	55.5	55.5	55.5	55
Domin Rep.					26	26	23-25	23-25	23-25
Turkey					99.5	99.5	99.5	99.5	99.5

avoid triggering the mandatory prepayment clause. As a result, an important part of rescheduling has been the granting of waivers to Chile to initiate its various debt reduction schemes (Chile's 1988 waivers and amendments that allowed other novel transactions are discussed later in this chapter).

Amendments and waivers by creditor banks enabled Chile to set up two formal main channels to accommodate the swapping of its medium- and long-term debt, beginning in June 1985[4]. The first of these channels is the country's Foreign Exchange Law, chapter XVIII conversions – to accommodate debt conversion by Chilean nationals. The second is chapter XIX *(loc. cit.)*– for debt conversion (i.e. debt-equity swaps or debt capitalisation) by foreign investors. There are also two less important formal channels – *D.L. 600* and chapter XVIII Annex 4 *(loc. cit.)*.

Under chapter XVIII, a Chilean national is permitted to acquire Chilean debt with a maturity of one year of more and negotiate its prepayment in pesos. This channel was established to allow Chilean entities (i.e. non-financial private sectors) to retire their own external indebtedness at a discount while providing a mechanism that circumvented the sharing provision of syndicated loans. In time it was seen to have much wider applications and became a channel for Chileans to repatriate their foreign assets (flight capital and foreign investments). Conversions under chapter XVIII contain the following restrictions:

i) No recourse to official foreign exchange markets to carry out such conversions. This provision is obviously important for private sectors wishing to reduce their foreign liabilities. The private sector thus has to obtain the necessary foreign exchange in the parallel market; the implications of this are discussed later in this section. On the other hand, by definition Chileans repatriating their foreign assets would already own their foreign exchange and would not use the official foreign exchange market.

ii) This conversion channel cannot be used by any public entities, banks or financial companies; it is only for the use of the non-financial private sector.

iii) There are limits to the volume of such conversions. In June 1985, the government set quotas; allocated these quotas to the commercial banks; the commercial banks gave the quotas to their existing borrowers; the borrowers used the parallel foreign exchange market to acquire foreign exchange; with their foreign exchange they acquired Chilean debt equivalent to their quota; and they used the purchased debt to retire their domestic debt with banking institutions. Later that year, the government realised the implicit value of these quotas (because of the discount on Chilean debt on the secondary market) and in September 1985 started auctioning them among banks. The volume to be auctioned bi-weekly was pre-set and averaged $20 million in the first eight months of 1987. Then, beginning in September 1987, the pre-setting of quota auction volume was abandoned. As a result the average volume jumped to $50-$60 million in the next six months. In March 1988, chapter XVIII was amended to permit certain mortgage debtors to amortize up to $6 000 of their debts with profits obtained from converting external debt bought at discount. This new feature put severe pressure on the parallel foreign exchange market, resulting in an immediate lowering of the volume of auctions in March 1988 followed by a suspension of auctions in May.

Under chapter XIX, this debt capitalisation channel enables foreigners to acquire Chilean debt to implement investments (through a conversion) in Chile. Conversions under chapter XIX, popularly known as debt-equity swaps, require prior approval of the Central

Bank of Chile. The proceeds of the swap would then be capitalised in the investment as agreed upon by the Central Bank. While the investor benefits from a portion of the discount on Chilean debt, there are some restrictions on the profits from these conversions. Thus:

i) for the first four years, profits must be reinvested in Chile;
ii) in the fifth year, repatriation of the first four years' profits may take place at a rate of 25 per cent per year;
iii) beginning in the fifth year, there are no restrictions on repatriation of profits generated from then on;
iv) the capital portion of the investment can be repatriated after ten years;
v) the investor has access to the *official* foreign exchange market for profit and capital repatriation when restrictions no longer apply; clearly the parallel market may be used at any time to circumvent restrictions [(i)-(iv)].

In September 1987, chapter XIX conversions were expanded to include investments in special closed-end funds. These funds require minimum captilisation of $20 million with 60 per cent or more invested in stocks and a minimum of 80 per cent in stocks and other long-term investments. Repatriation restrictions are somewhat more stringent for these conversions. Profits may be repatriated after six years without any restrictions and only 20 per cent of the accumulated profits of the first six years can be repatriated at that time. Capital repatriation is permitted after twelve years. Access to the official foreign exchange market is allowed when restrictions are moved.

The channel available through D.L. 600, one of the less formal channels, is the foreign investment statute of Chile. D.L. 600 conversions differ from regular chapter XIX because they are in cash. After the investments are made, they are governed by the same restrictions as chapter XIX. Conversions under chapter XVIII Annex 4 are a specific subset of chapter XVIII: namely, the acquisition by a Chilean national of Chilean external debt for conversion into an equity position.

Informal Debt Reduction Schemes

In view of the large discount on Chilean debt, private sector debtors have a powerful incentive to buy back their own debt on the secondary market, using the parallel foreign exchange market. This method has been used mainly by non-financial entities in Chile because of the close supervision of financial institutions. This category of conversion is termed as "other" by the Central Bank.

Hedging and Other Policies

In its April 1988 renegotiation with creditors, Chile acquired new policy options for its debt management. Two possibilities have already resulted from these renegotiations. First is the opportunity for Chile to hedge the exchange and interest rate exposures on its external debt. Second is the opportunity to use cash as collateral to securitise old debt and access new money.

The real burden of Chilean debt, which is mostly dollar-denominated, is always changing because of wide fluctuations in exchange rates. Since about 80 per cent of Chilean debt exists on a floating basis, interest rate fluctuations also add to the burden of debt-servicing. While Chile may believe that market efficiency translates in the long run into currency and interest rate movements cancelling each other out (i.e. interest rate parity and foreign exchange market efficiency), various instruments like interest rates and currency swaps provide low-cost hedging techniques. As a result, after the 1988 renegotiations Chile has started to use $150 million (known as the lien basket) for hedging operations that have affected about $2 billion of external obligations. These operations and the possibilities have been summarised for the Central Bank of Chile by Mr. Garces (1988):

> "Until some time ago, Banco Central managed only international assets, that is, its foreign currency reserves. Last year it issued rules on operations in futures, caps, collars, options, etc., as regards interest rates, and on currency swaps and futures, even hedging against the risk inherent in commodities markets. These events are also the beginning of a policy for gradual utilization of all instruments available on the international markets for managing the foreign liabilities caused by debt. This field of innovation in foreign debt management has been recognized as such by the World Bank and other international organizations, and should be a point of interest and cooperation with debtor countries on the part of the international creditor banking community."
>
> Certainly, these instruments are not designed to resolve the problem of acute over-indebtedness; however, in conjunction with a broad range of additional instruments included in a menu of alternatives, they may help to alleviate substantial exchange differentials or higher outlays, and payments because of interest rates rising sharply at pricing time. By way of example, the currency differential between 1985 and 1987 meant more than US$1 billion for the country, and we know that a difference of one point in variable interest means US$160 million. The advantage of these financial instruments currently offered by the international markets is that they help to make foreign debt management more predictable and rational. As a result, major savings may attend foreign currency transfers abroad, resulting from variations or disturbances in interest or exchange rates.

A broad strategy for liability management should comprise currency diversification, interest rate hedging, interest rate diversification into fixed and variable rates, followed later by variety and choice of liability instruments and maturity diversification. Lastly, a joint strategy for managing liabilities and assets should be harmonized to fulfil the same objectives of various kinds of risk reduction: to limit costs and ensure creditworthiness and stability in foreign relations.

The second innovation, the use of cash collateral for securitising old debt and getting new money, operates under the following principles:

i) any pre-payment of foreign currency-denominated debt must be offered to all creditors on a *pro rata* basis;

ii) any such transaction requires the two-thirds (for public debtors) and one-half (private debtors) approval of Chile's creditors – on a weighted basis;

iii) repayments in peso need not be offered on a *pro rata* basis (as that would not trigger the sharing or mandatory repayment clause); and

iv) buy-backs are to be funded by no more than $500 million from the Copper Stabilisation Fund.

Apparently serious debt renegotiations can result in a broader menu of options for effective debt management policies. This is an evolutionary process and Chile has used it quite successfully.

Public Debt Conversions

Although the focus of Chilean debt reduction through conversions has been on the private sector, public sector debt reduction has also been significant.

Public sector debt repurchases have had two channels – chapter XVIII and informal negotiations.

Impact of Conversions and Repurchases on the Size of Chilean Debt

In Table 2.2, the impact of the various channels on the reduction of financial and non-financial private sector debt is shown. Table 2.3 contains reductions in public sector debt and in Table 2.4 the reduction for both private and public sector debt is given by year.

Several facts stand out from these data. First, the bulk of debt reductions are in the private sector. Second, the formal channels – chapter XVIII and chapter XIX – provide the major source of debt reduction. Third, the financial private sector has been the biggest contributor (as opposed to the non-financial private sector). Its contribution has come from formal channels (instead of the non-financial sector's informal ones), basically because it is closely supervised by the Central Bank. Fourth, these figures may be misleading regarding the role of the non-financial sector. Specifically, in Table 2.2, there appears to be no capitalisation of private non-financial assets. This may not be exact because, even though under chapter XIX there were no conversions that reduced private non-financial debt, the proceeds of other conversions were used to invest in the private non-financial sector. This area of investment is not clear from the tables (Larrain, 1986*b*).

These conversions have greatly affected Chilean debt, most visibly in the case of private sector debt owed to commercial banks (see Table 2.5). As expected, the impact has been strongest on commercial debt. From the lower half of this table several points stand out. First, as mentioned earlier in this chapter, private sector (financial) debt shifted from being non-guaranteed by the government in 1982 to largely guaranteed in 1988. Second, financial private sector debt with commercial banks declined from $4 971 million to $3 128.7 million, for a reduction of 37.1 per cent; while non-financial private sector debt

Table 2.2. PRIVATE DEBT REDUCTION

US$ million, accumulated as of June 1, 1988

	Financial Sector	Non-financial Sector	Total
Chapter XVIII	1 114.4	0.0	1 114.4
Chapter XVIII – Annex 4	39.6	53.2	92.8
Chapter XIX	762.3	1.2	763.5
Capitalisation – DL 600	139.8	94.1	233.9
Portfolio swaps	45.1	3.3	48.4
Other	42.8	610.8	653.6
Total	2 144.0	762.6	2 966.6

Source: Central Bank of Chile.

Table 2.3. THE REPURCHASE OF PUBLIC DEBT

US$ million, accumulated as of June 1, 1988

	Financial sector		Non-financial	Total
	Central Bank	Banco del Estado		
Chapter XVIII	226.1	153.5	162.4	542.0
Condonations, direct repurchases and other	0.0	0.0	281.0	281.0
Total	226.1	153.5	443.4	823.0

Source: Central Bank of Chile.

decreased from $2 784.7 million to $1 048.7 million, for a reduction of 62.4 per cent; and overall private sector debt with commercial banks declined from $7 755.7 million to $4 177.4 million, for a reduction of 46.25 per cent. The reduction of $3 578.3 million in the private sector's commercial bank debt parallels the contribution of private sector conversions – which amounted to $2 906.6 million over the same period (see Table 2.2).

The figures for public sector debt are shown in Table 2.6, and as expected, this kind of debt with commercial banks has increased since 1982, from $3 490 million to $7 656.7 million. The contribution of public sector conversions (Table 2.3) of $823 million is less significant – 10.7 per cent of outstanding public sector debt – than that of the private sector.

Table 2.4. TOTAL (PRIVATE AND PUBLIC) DEBT REDUCTION

Millions of US$ and % of total debt

	1985	1986	1987	1988[1]	Total	
					US$ M	%
Chapter XVIII[2]	115.2	410.6	695.8	527.6	1 749.2	41.0
Chapter XIX	25.9	217.0	711.5	252.1	1 206.5	28.8
Capitalisations – DL 600	53.0	56.3	124.6	0.0	233.9	5.6
Portfolio swaps	41.0	27.2	0.0	0.0	68.2	1.6
Other[3]	88.7	275.9	451.0	119.0	934.6	22.3
Total	323.8	987.0	1 982.9	898.7	4 192.4	100.0
Accumulated Total	323.8	1 310.8	3 293.7	4 192.4	4 192.4	

1. As of June 30.
2. Includes Chapter XVIII and Chapter XIX, Annex 4.
3. Includes direct operations and condonations.

Source: Central Bank of Chile.

Table 2.5. MEDIUM- AND LONG-TERM PRIVATE DEBT BY CREDITOR

US$ million, year end

	1982	1983	1984	1985	1986	1987	1988[2]
Multilateral Institutions	0.0	0.0	10.9	19.0	23.5	75.0	76.3
Government Agencies	13.2	10.7	9.6	8.1	14.6	25.3	29.2
Commercial Banks	7 755.7	7 372.8	7 344.6	6 463.5	5 692.9	4 225.0	4 177.4
Suppliers[1]	443.2	326.4	252.6	166.9	175.3	245.2	258.8
Other[1]	445.7	432.3	445.2	472.2	463.3	569.5	587.1
Total	8 567.8	8 142.2	8 062.9	7 129.7	6 369.6	5 140.0	5 128.8

MEDIUM- AND LONG-TERM PRIVATE DEBT WITH COMMERCIAL BANKS

	1982	1983	1984	1985	1986	1987	1988[2]
Financial Sector							
Guaranteed	0.0	1 401.0	1 700.8	1 995.1	2 928.8	2 699.5	2 943.7
Non-guaranteed	4 971.0	3 394.1	3 368.7	2 960.6	1 296.0	501.6	185.0
Non-financial Sector	2 784.7	2 577.6	2 275.1	1 777.8	1 468.1	1 053.9	1 048.7
Total	7 755.7	7 372.8	7 344.6	6 463.5	5 692.9	4 225.0	4 177.4

1. Suppliers' debt and "other" debt belong only to the non-financial sector.
2. As of May 31, 1988.
Source: Central Bank of Chile.

Overall the total contribution of conversions to Chile's commercial debt is impressive: \$4 192.4 million (Table 2.4), while Chile's total outstanding commercial debt stood at \$11 834.1 million in June 1988. Moreover, the contribution did not stop there. In November 1988, for instance, after receiving bids, the government bought back \$299 million of foreign bank debt for \$168 million (using the Copper Stabilisation Fund) for an average discount of 44 per cent.

Issues Raised by the Chilean Debt Reduction Schemes

While Chile's debt reduction programmes have undoubtedly been effective in reducing commercial debt, they raise the following important issues:

- problems with domestic macro-economic management;
- benefits to Chile versus investors;
- additionality of conversions;
- future potential;
- efficient debt reduction.

These issues are addressed in the next sections.

Table 2.6. MEDIUM- AND LONG-TERM PUBLIC AND TOTAL DEBT BY CREDITOR

US$ million, year end

	Multilateral Institutions		Governement Agencies		Commercial Banks		Suppliers[1]		Total	
	Public	Total	Public	Total	Public	Total	Public	Total	Public	Total
1982	444.4	444.4	820.4	833.6	3 490.0	11 246.7	402.0	846.2	5 156.8	13 814.6
1983	645.1	645.1	790.8	801.5	4 945.7	12 318.5	307.7	634.1	6 689.3	14 831.5
1984	935.4	946.3	606.1	615.7	7 093.9	14 438.5	264.9	517.5	8 900.3	16 963.2
1985	1 425.3	1 444.3	629.6	637.7	8 250.8	14 714.3	214.5	381.4	10 620.2	17 649.9
1986	1 964.9	1 928.4	755.0	769.6	8 434.8	14 127.7	355.4	524.5	11 450.1	17 813.5
1987	2 418.1	2 493.1	696.7	722.0	8 442.5	12 667.5	497.8	738.6	12 055.1	17 190.7
1988[1]	2 518.1	2 594.4	708.2	732.1	7 658.7	11 834.1	510.1	765.2	11 393.1	18 512.9

MEDIUM- AND LONG-TERM PUBLIC DEBT WITH COMMERCIAL BANKS

	Financial Sector	Non-Financial Sector	Total
1982	1 003.2	2 486.8	3 490.0
1983	2 461.9	2 483.8	4 945.7
1984	4 386.4	2 707.5	7 093.9
1985	5 201.8	3 049.0	8 250.8
1986	5 521.6	2 913.2	8 434.8
1987	5 628.5	2 814.0	8 442.5
1988[1]	5 315.6	2 341.1	7 656.7

1. As of May 31st, 1988.
Source: Central Bank of Chile.

Macro-Management and Debt Reduction

A conversion has important domestic financial implications. A private sector debtor would have to borrow pesos or use liquid peso assets[5]. For public debt, the Central Bank could expand the money supply, causing inflation; borrow in the domestic market, raising interest rates; or use its foreign reserves. The Central Bank has used foreign exchange sparingly (Copper Stabilisation Fund) and has not expanded the money supply. Instead,

Table 2.7. DOMESTIC REAL INTEREST RATES
Per cent

	90 to 365 days	1 to 3 years
1985		
June	8.73	8.57
July	7.58	7.61
August	7.88	7.38
September	7.67	5.91
October	7.39	5.61
November	6.87	5.67
December	6.22	6.76
1986		
January	5.93	5.24
February	5.37	5.23
March	5.12	5.59
April	4.61	5.34
May	4.45	4.47
June	3.92	4.69
July	3.61	4.25
August	3.40	3.69
September	3.28	4.51
October	3.15	4.09
November	3.28	4.41
December	3.47	4.24
1987		
January	3.57	4.13
February	3.51	4.83
March	3.76	4.35
April	3.94	4.64
May	4.04	4.93
June	4.37	5.15
July	4.28	3.98
August	4.29	5.39
September	4.76	5.18
October	5.12	5.75
November	4.85	5.38
December	4.46	4.87

Source: Central Bank of Chile.

both the private and public sector have resorted to peso borrowing – putting latent upward pressure on domestic interest rates. The Central Bank issued debt amounting to 9.9 per cent of its liabilities as of December 1987 in connection with these operations (Larrain 1988*b*).

Chile has, however, been able to avoid pressures on interest rates. In fact both short- and long-term interest rates have declined (see Table 2.7). The reasons for this are:

i) public sector deficit as a percentage of GDP has fallen;
ii) the 1984 tax reform induced more equity financing, rather than debt;
iii) enhanced liquidity of the firms;
iv) growing supply of long-term funds from pension funds; and
v) increased financial intermediation (Larrain, 1988*b*).

A particular use of debt conversion is its support of government privatisation policy. In the first place, conversion for privatisation does not influence interest rates or inflation since the government is the seller. In fact, privatisation through swaps may ameliorate interest rates and inflation because most public sector enterprises lose money; thus, its sale may help government finances. Second, privatisation through conversion may avoid many of the usual political pitfalls: since the sale price of most government enterprises is below cost, its sale carries political recriminations. Conversions, though, allow the government to sell its assets at a higher domestic price instead of taking a larger part of the available secondary market discount. Chile had privatised five public enterprises by mid 1988; the face value of these transactions was $79.5 million.

The purchase (as opposed to conversion) of a country's debt requires foreign exchange. Besides using official foreign exchange reserves and foreign access of the private sector, another option is to obtain the needed foreign exchange on the parallel market (full convertibility was suspended in 1982 in Chile), increasing the demand for foreign exchange. Transactions on this market have ranged between about $60 to $100 million per month. Such purchases would result in a depreciation of the peso on the parallel market, affecting the exchange rate gap.

In Table 2.8, this gap (the percentage difference between the parallel and official) is shown. It narrowed from about 18 per cent to approximately 5 per cent by late 1987, while the volume of debt repurchases increased. The reason for this unexpected development appears to be the differential between domestic and foreign interest rates. The lower foreign interest rates are, compared to domestic rates, the more incentive there is for holding pesos, and less pressure is put on the parallel foreign exchange market. Up to late 1987, this effect seems to have more than compensated for the repurchase of foreign debt, thereby reducing the exchange rate gap (see Larrain, 1988*b*). However, as noted earlier in this chapter, in early 1988 the demand for mortgage conversion operations tightly squeezed the parallel exchange market, resulting in a suspension of Central Bank auctions.

One of the major tools for controlling the exchange rate gap is bi-monthly auctions. They have been one of Central Bank's key policy instruments. Their most dramatic application was in early 1988 when the authorities suspended auctions after the premium in the parallel market surpassed 10 per cent. The reasons for avoiding a high premium in the parallel market are several:

i) it increases expectations of a devaluation that encourage speculation (the memories of this occurring in the early 1980s are still vivid in Chile);
ii) it raises incentives for under-(exports) and over-(imports) invoicing and smuggling; and

Table 2.8. THE EXCHANGE RATE GAP

	Official Rate[1] (ch$/US$)	Parallel Rate[2] (ch$/US$)	Exchange Rate Gap (%)
1985			
June	155.49	183.3	17.9
July	170.52	191.4	12.2
August	173.16	200.5	15.8
September	174.74	214.7	22.9
October	175.95	209.5	19.1
November	177.49	208.6	17.5
December	179.21	204.0	13.8
Year average			(17.0)
1986			
January	181.17	202.1	11.6
February	183.15	202.4	10.5
March	185.81	199.6	7.4
April	187.19	197.9	5.7
May	189.26	196.6	3.9
June	190.89	198.7	4.1
July	191.92	199.6	4.0
August	193.57	205.3	6.1
September	194.73	213.2	9.5
October	195.80	219.0	11.8
November	198.06	214.2	6.1
December	200.39	211.7	3.9
Year average			(7.1)
1987			
January	206.65	211.6	4.4
February	205.25	214.6	4.6
March	208.61	220.5	5.7
April	211.48	222.6	5.3
May	214.63	225.5	5.1
June	218.32	230.4	5.5
July	220.35	232.7	5.6
August	221.66	235.5	5.3
September	224.25	235.5	5.0
October	226.82	239.5	5.6
November	229.85	244.2	6.2
December	232.65	243.5	4.6
Year average			(5.2)

1. Official rate corresponds to *dollar acuerdo.*
2. All figures are monthly averages.

Source: Central Bank of Chile (Larrain, 1988*b*).

iii) it induces other negative economic developments, ultimately resulting in a loss of business confidence.

In sum, macro-economic problems resulting from debt reduction schemes are very much determined by overall economic conditions. First, if the government's domestic budgetary situation is in balance, it is easier to accommodate conversions, avoiding higher interest rates and inflation. Second, if the official exchange rate is close to the parallel rate, repurchase of foreign debt would not cause the two rates to diverge, and speculation would be avoided. Third, if domestic interest rates reflect credit conditions (avoiding too high or too low real rates), demand for domestic currency assets will continue, again easing pressure on the parallel foreign exchange market. Fourth, the ownership of substantial foreign assets by nationals could be a good source of debt reduction. Although Chile's private foreign assets are not high compared with other Latin American debt, Chile had had remarkable success in tapping this source of funds.

Another way to look at the macro-economic effects of a swap is to compare an investment through a swap to a regular foreign direct investment. Bergsman and Edisis (1988) have done this and they conclude that it depends on whether the swap is "additional" or not (a discussion of additionality appears later in this work). Bergsman and Edisis state:

> "Any investment made through the swap program implies that the government prepays foreign debt, at a discount identical to that which it charges the foreign investor in the swap transaction. If the investment was additional, the effect on the government is to use local currency to pay for the debt reduction, at the same interest rates, greater fiscal effort, and/or reduced consumption. If the investment was not additional, then the prepayment of the foreign debt was in effect done with foreign exchange – and the swap program has not added any "cost" in terms of inflationay effect, etc. Note that allowing a transaction through a swap always results in reducing foreign debt; it can cost the government *either* foreign exchange *or* the need to come up with domestic currency, *but not both.* Also, *if the swap investment is not additional then the swap program does not add to inflationary pressures.* These two criticisms that are often leveled at swap programs – lack of additionality, and inflationary impact – logically cannot apply simultaneously. A swap program leads to inflationary impacts only to the extent that investment made through it would not have happened if there were not swap programs".

The Accrual of Benefits of Debt Discount

One of the major benefits of debt reduction through debt repurchase and debt conversion is capturing the available discount on the secondary market.

What makes debt repurchase and conversion attractive is the discount on the debt's face value. The question is, who captures it, the debtor or the creditor (investor)? There are four cases that should be assessed: public sector debt repurchase under chapter XVIII, private sector debt repurchase under chapter XVIII, public sector debt conversion under chapter XIX and private sector debt conversion under chapter XIX.

We have mentioned that the Central Bank repurchased its own debt through the issuance of peso-denominated long-term bonds. Table 2.9 shows the behaviour or redemption price over time; this price sets a floor for private debt redemption. Table 2.10 shows the discount (both public and private) that Chile has captured on chapter XVIII repurchases. Larrain (1988*b*) has summarised the result:

> *i)* "The Central Bank initially started these operations allocating monthly cupos to local banks in proportion to their capital; this did not produce any revenue. Later on, since September 1985, the Central Bank started to auction the cupos, and thus

Table 2.9. CONDITIONS OF REDEMPTION FOR CENTRAL BANK DEBT

Debt Repurchases under Chapter XVIII

	Nominal Redemption (% of par value)	Real Interest Rate (%)	Years to Maturity	Value of bond[2] (%)	Effective Redemption (%)
April 1986[1]	97	TIP – 0.5	10	96.0	93.12
June 1987	97	TIP – 0.5	10	93.0	90.20
September 1987	92	TIP – 1.1	6	91.5	84.18
October 1987	88	TIP – 1.65	6	89.7	79.00
December 1987	92	TIP – 1.1	6	91.2	83.00

1. No bonds were issued pior to this date.
2. Estimated present value of the bond.
3. Redemptions could be done in dollar-linked bonds up to September 1987, but no foreign creditor opted for this alternative.

Source: Central Bank of Chile and private financial intermediaries. (Larrain, 1988b).

Table 2.10. ESTIMATED DISTRIBUTION OF DISCOUNTS ON DEBT REPURCHASE OPERATIONS[1]

% and US$ million

	1985	1986	1987
Total discount over par[2]	32.0	31.2	35.7
Central Bank fee[3]	2.7	10.9	20.5
Redemption discount[4]	8.0	9.0	12.0
Cost of parallel market premium[5]	11.6	4.9	3.3
Other	8.7	6.4	–0.1
Formal debt repurchases (US$ million)	115.2	410.6	695.8
Total debt repurchases (US$ million)	203.5	686.5	1 147.2

1. Figures are year averages except for 1985 when they refer only to the second semester (after formal debt reduction operations started in Chile).
2. From Vatnick (1988) and data of Merril Lynch and Shearson Lehman. Discounts are averages between buying and selling prices of public and publicly guaranteed debt. Thus, they reflect accurately the situation of private financial debt, but can serve, at debt, only as rough, order-of-magnitude estimators of the discounts on private non-financial debt.
3. Value of fees divided by the total face value of formal transactions, including operations under Chapter XVIII, Annex 4.
4. From Aninat y Mendez (1986), Germines (1986, 1987), Central Bank of Chile and market sources.
5. Expressed as a percentage of par value.

Source: Larrain, 1988b.

to capture part of the secondary market discount. From a low 2.7 points captured on average in 1985, the Bank has increased its share to over 20 points in 1987.

ii) In addition to the Central Bank's fee, conversions of debt certificates are done in local currency at less than par value. These redemptions discounts captured directly by debtors have also increased, from 8 per cent in 1985 to around 11 per cent in 1987.

iii) Since the country is not allowing access to its international reserves to finance these operations, it has to attract offshore assets of domestic residents. The way to lure these back is to offer a premium over the official exchange. Thus, this gap is the price paid to obtain parallel dollars. Since redemptions are done at the official rate, the gap eats a portion of the discount. Interestingly, the cost of this premium has declined in spite of the increased volume of operations, from 11.6 per cent in 1985 to 3.3 per cent in 1987. Of course, this does not indicate any cause-effect relationship between these variables.

The rest of the discount goes to cover intermediaries' fees and other miscellaneous costs. This has suffered a sharp decline. From the viewpoint of the country, we can say that the total discount captured is the sum of the Central Bank fee plus the redemption discount. In 1985 this amounted to less than one-third of the secondary market discount (10.7 per cent out of 32 per cent); two years later it had reached about 90 per cent of the discount (32.5 points out of 35.7). Thus the country has been capturing an increasing portion of debt discounts through repurchase operations."

As Larrain (1988*b*) has shown, the attractiveness of debt repurchases for the private sector lies in the profit that can be made on the transaction.

profit = $(p - f)\, e - p'\, e'$

where: p = Redemption price of Chilean debt

p' = Purchase price of Chilean debt

e = Official exchange rate (applicable to redemption)

e' = Parallel market exchange rate

f = Central Bank fee

over time, profits tend to decline to zero, thus:

$$\frac{p - f}{p'} = \frac{e'}{e}$$

resulting in the convergence of the size of the Central Bank fee and premium in the parallel foreign exchange market. Given eventual changes, this means that the market for debt repurchase has grown more competitive. Unfortunately, the increasingly higher exchange rate premium diminishes the discount obtained by Chile.

The situation is different for debt conversions (chapter XIX). The effective redemption price (shown in Table 2.11) set by the Central Bank for debt again clearly shows the way for redemption of private sector debt. The discount captured by Chile on debt conversion (public sector and private financial sector) is shown in Table 2.12. With a similar redemption price to that of chapter XVIII and in the absence of Central Bank fees, most of the discount is captured by the foreign investor who gets a substantial subsidy as a per cent of his dollar investment; while Chile gets only about 30 per cent of the available discount, even less in earlier years.

Evidently the use of auctions to set redemption price of the debt can allow the government to gain a larger share of the secondary market discount. Bergsman and Edisis (1988) concluded from their analysis that four policies would enhance the share of discount obtained by the debtor government[6]:

- use auctions to set redemption price;
- allow domestic participants;
- do not exclude too many applicants;
- do not require fresh money with the conversion.

Additionality

One of the primary questions concerning the desirability of debt reduction schemes is the issue of additionality (see Dornbusch, 1987). Debt reduction schemes are fully additional when they induce investments that would not have occurred without the schemes. This definition, however, may not be complete. For instance, a debt reduction transaction may be fully additional in the above sense yet stimulate higher domestic interest rates and other negative effects that eventually reduce other investments (both foreign and domestic). And although a particular debt reduction transaction may be fully additional today, it may be undertaken without a debt reduction scheme tomorrow (i.e. zero future additionality). Therefore should additionality be measured at a certain point or over time? Another aspect of measuring additionality is whether the incentive afforded to the investor through the available discount is the cheapest alternative to inducing foreign investment. In short, additionality is a difficult concept to define, let alone measure and quantify.

Table 2.11. CONDITIONS OF REDEMPTION FOR CENTRAL BANK DEBT

Debt Capitalisations under Chapter XIX

	Nominal Redemption[1] (% of par value)	Real Interest Rate[1] (%)	Years to Maturity[1]	Value of bond[2] (%)	Effective Redemption (%)
December 1985	100	TIP – 0.5	15	100.0[3]	n.a.
May 1986	100	TIP – 1.5	8	91.0	91.0
		TIP – 1.0	10		
		TIP – 0.5	15		
August 1987	100	TIP – 1.1	15	83.6	83.6
October 1987	100	TIP – 1.65	15	79.0	79.0
December 1987	100	TIP – 1.1	15	83.6	83.6

1. Conditions only apply to bonds effectively issued by the Central Bank.
2. Secondary market value of the Central Bank bond.
3. There are no representative data available.

Source: Central Bank of Chile and private financial intermediaries. (Larrain, 1988b).

Table 2.12. ESTIMATED DISTRIBUTION OF DISCOUNTS ON CHILEAN FOREIGN DEBT: CHAPTER XIX[1]

Per cent

	1985	1986	1987
Total discount[2]	32.0	31.2	35.7
Central Bank fee	–	–	–
Redemption discount[2]	(8.0)	(9.0)	(12.0)
Intermediaries fees[3]	(2.0)	(2.0)	(2.0)
Subsidy to foreign investor (points of par value)	(22.0)	(20.2)	(21.7)
Subsidy to foreign investor (% of dollar investment)	32.4	29.4	33.7

1. Figures are year averages, except for 1985, when these include only the second half of the year.
2. Same as Table 2.10.
3. Rough estimates, based on Aninat and Mendez (1986) and market sources.

Source: Larrain, 1988b.

With the above reservations, what can be said about additionality in terms of the Chilean experience? Table 2.13 lists the reductions in external debt by various channels. Additionality obviously does not apply to any of the debt repurchase operations (chapter XVIII and chapter XVIII Annex 4). These transactions are essentially discounted debt buy-backs that use foreign exchange (from official and private sources). Similarly, the other category of reduction schemes in Table 2.13 – basically the buy-back of their own debt by private debtors through the parallel exchange market (informal debt reduction) – is essentially a repurchase operation. Capitalisation transactions using D.L. 600 (cash investments) are again not the subject of additionality. The most important issue in debt repurchase is not additionality but whether it is efficient debt reduction.

Thus, the amount of Chilean debt reduction that applies to additionality (narrowly defined as the amount that would not have occurred without conversion schemes) is found under chapter XIX and portfolio swaps. This amount under chapter XIX is $443.0 million for the public sector and $763.5 million for the private, or a total of $1 206.5 million; under the portfolio swap programme it is $19.8 million for the public sector and $48.4 million for the private, a total of $68.2 million. The question of basic additionality, then, is what proportion of this $1 274.7 million in investments in Chile (direct and portfolio) would have taken place without debt reduction plans?

A definitive answer to even this simple question is difficult. However, an insight can be gained by some rough assessment. If commercial bank creditors swapped debt for equity assets for their own portfolio, this can safely be assumed to be additional. Banks do not normally take non-financial equity positions, especially in developing countries. However, swaps for their own account (if they do not require infusion of new money) may help reduce their obligations for fresh money in rescheduling agreements. Banks, however, would not swap loans for equity position unless they were unhappy about the current and future potential of the debt obligation they own (see Bergsman and Edisis 1988 for more details)[7]. All in all, bank investment in Chile would probably not have occurred unless Chilean debt was selling at a discount and Chile had a programme in place. Chapter XIX investments

Table 2.13. EXTERNAL DEBT REDUCTION BY DEBTOR AND MECHANISM[1]

Millions of US$, accumulated as of June 1988

	Debt Repurchase		Debt Capitalisation		Portfolio Swaps	Other	Total	
	Chapter XVIII	Chapter XIX Annex 4	Chapter XIX	Capitalisation DL 600			US$	%
Public Sector	542.0	0.0	443.0	0.0	19.8	281.0	1 286.8	30.7
Financial	379.6	0.0	384.0	0.0	17.8	0.0	781.4	18.6
Central Bank	226.1	0.0	342.4	0.0	12.4	0.0	580.9	
Banco del Estado	163.5	0.0	41.6	0.0	5.4	0.0	200.5	
Non financial	162.4	0.0	59.0	0.0	2.0	281.0	564.4	12.0
Private Sector	1 114.4	92.8	763.6	233.9	48.4	653.6	2 900.6	69.3
Financial	1 114.4	39.6	762.3	139.8	45.1	42.8	2 144.04	61.1
With public guarantee			302.2	0.0	22.4	0.0	743.4	
No public guarantee			460.1	139.8	22.7	42.8	1 400.6	
Non financial	0.0	53.2	1.2	94.1	3.3	610.8	762.6	10.2
Total	1 656.4	92.8	1 206.5	233.9	60.2	934.6	4 192.4	100.0

1. Accumulated as of December 1987.

Source: Central Bank of Chile. (Larrain, 1988b).

authorised for banks and bank subsidiaries amount to approximately US$ 1 billion, representing about 38 per cent of total amount permitted up to 30 June 1989 and representing about 57 operations (27.27 per cent of total approved operations).

Simple additionality applies to conversion by private investors and multinational corporations – i.e. non-bank investors. Bergsman and Edisis (1988) have shed substantial light on this through interviews with multinational corporation investors in Chile, and have concluded that 64 per cent of the conversions (non-creditor bank) in the interview sample were additional in the case of Chile. Conversions potentially reduce the basis of new money at the time of bank renegotiations, though this negative effect of conversions may be small considering new money may not be readily available.

Thus, if 27.27 per cent of chapter XIX was bank conversions (fully additional), this results in a high level of additionality for 74.02 per cent of the total (including bank conversions)[8]. Bergsman and Edisis concluded that in fact the level of additionality was higher in Chile than in the other countries studied – Argentina (45 per cent), Mexico (44 per cent) and Brazil (0 per cent). They proposed the following steps to augment opportunities for additionality:

i) keep investor incentive strong;
ii) maintain programme continuity;
iii) during the screening process, encourage export-oriented manufacturing activities, banks and other conversions, and eliminate obvious non-additional investment[9];
iv) be reasonable in restricting dividend and capital repatriation.

Although additionality is a desirable attribute of a conversion scheme, a non-additional conversion may not necessarily be undesirable. A debt-equity swap is best compared to a direct foreign investment. When $100 million of this kind of investment is compared to $100 million (face value) of investment through a debt-equity swap in Chile, what is the foreign exchange difference to Chile?[10]. If Chilean debt is selling at a 50 per cent discount on the secondary market, a conversion will reduce the debt by $100 million and result in a national investment. If the $100 million capital flowed into Chile, then Chile could have used it to repurchase $200 million of its debt. Thus Chile would have had the investment, as in the case of the debt-equity swap, but it would have reduced its debt by an extra $100 million. In this simple example we have assumed that the investor captured all the discount. If Chile had captured it instead, then the investor would have needed $200 million of Chilean debt (face value) to make his $100 million in investment. If this was so there would be no difference between the two cases: although the conversion was not additional, Chile would be much more interested in a direct foreign investment. In essence, the net foreign exchange impact of additionality is directly tied to who captures the discount. Successful capture minimizes the negative effects of non-additionality. In this elementary comparison we have assumed that a direct foreign investment of $100 million resulted in $100 million of foreign exchange inflow. In practice this is much less, as a multinational corporation imports its equipment and may also borrow in the local capital market.

Efficient Debt Reduction

Debt-equity swaps basically transform an external debt into an equity position in the debtor country. Whether the debtor country's obligations in the form of external transfers (interest and principal in the case of debt or profits and capital in the case of equity), will be reduced depends on several factors – the distribution of secondary market discounts between debtor and creditor, the timing of debt-servicing (affected by interest rates and reschedulings), the time-frame for profit and capital repatriation, and the rate of discount applied to both external payment profiles. In a sense the efficient way to deal with debt management and in turn debt reduction policies is to diminish the present discounted value of foreign exchange outflows linked to future debt-servicing and profit and capital repatriation. Before discussing this issue, two related issues should be addressed.

Besides the central issue of discounted value of external obligations, there are two arguments in favour of swaps. One that favours equity financing claims that profit and capital repatriation are easier for a country because they depend on the health of the economy; debt-servicing is much more dependent on external factors. Larrain (1988*b*) has correctly noted that for Chile the issue is the timing of profit repatriation, which depends on profit generation and profit reinvestment (both of which depend on the domestic business cycle). Thus, the behaviour of profit repatriation depends on which of these forces (profit repatriation or reinvestment) is more pro-cyclical. Larrain's results show on the one hand that swaps, rather than debt, provide easier servicing of obligation (non pro-cyclical). On the other hand, equity financing carries a substantially higher cost in terms of outflows (even after accounting for the discount on debt conversion).

The second argument that has traditionally favoured direct foreign investment and thus swaps is their ancillary benefits. Capital and foreign exchange are only a few of their attributes; they also provide opportunities for technology, patents, trademarks, training, management, access to foreign markets and the like. Thus the argument for conversion cannot be based purely on discounted values of obligations under debt and equity financing. Unfortunately, direct foreign investments in Chile declined sharply at the onset of the debt crisis. They had reached $385 million in 1982, then fell to $129 million (1983), $67 million (1984), $62 million (1985), and to $57 million in 1986 before recovering to $98 million in 1987[11]. One reason for this is Chile's domestic economic and external debt-servicing problem, which obviously increases investment risk. A possibility exists that conversion may have partly replaced traditional direct foreign investment – i.e. non-additionality; this argument is, however, weakened from a glance at the figures from the 1987 recovery, the year with the most conversions. We will lay aside these other benefits to turn to the issue of efficient debt reduction.

To Sachs (1989), debt reduction is "a restructuring of the outstanding debt in a way that reduces the expected present discounted value of the contractual obligations of the debtor." By this definition, debt reduction is not simply repaying principal. It must include an easing of the present discounted value of debt repayment. Thus debt reduction in Sachs' view implies "a rescheduling of debt at sub-market interest rates; a cancellation of part of principal; exit bonds with sub-market interest rates; a buy-back of debt at discount relative to face value; etc."[12].

To Larrain (1988*b*), optimal debt reduction encompasses the above but includes another dimension. Relying on the analysis of Jorgenson and Sachs (1988), Larrain examines the debt experience of Chile in the 1930s. He compares Chile and other countries that suspended debt payments (Bolivia, Colombia and Peru) to Argentina, which did not. Chile's present discounted value of payments was below that of Argentina's (see Table 2.14). Moreover, Larrain argues that Argentina did not receive other benefits (such as new money) from being a "model" debtor in this period. He attributes Chile's success to generalised suspension of payments, decline in exports, the linking of unilateral payments to export performance and no additional cost of payment suspension, since Chile had already lost access to commercial credit. Larrain claims that settlement timing in a debt dispute is

Table 2.14. DEBT RELIEF AND ACCESS TO CREDIT IN THE 1930s

	Present Value of repayments / Present Value of borrowings	External Finance / Exports
Argentina	1.25	9.161
Bolivia	0.54	36.502
Chile	0.56	13.792
Colombia	0.85	8.055
Peru	0.52	15.685

Notes: Column 1: Refers to all dollar bonds issued between 1922 and 1930.
Column 2: Average for the period 1950-1964.
Source: Jorgenson and Sachs (1988).

important in determining the final cost (in present value terms) of settlement with creditors (see Table 2.15).

This argument clearly would open a new avenue of debt policy for Chile; specifically suspension of debt payments, if it were not for the belief that such actions damage debtor relations with creditor governments and international institutions – which are a growing source of financing to fill the gap in commercial credit.

Our approach to debt reduction discussed both in Chapter 1 and the concluding chaptes of this study has been very similar to that of Sachs. However, the obvious should be stressed. In any debt renegotiation, Chile should obtain the best possible discounted terms on debt repayment. In any debt repurchase or debt conversion, Chile should capture the largest share of available discount.

Table 2.15. DEBT RELIEF AND THE TIMING OF SETTLEMENTS

	Principal Outstanding[1]	Present Value of Repayment[1]	Present Value Ratio (post-default)	Year of Final Settlement with Creditors
Bolivia	59.42	4.63	0.08	1958
Chile	260.73	80.39	0.31	1948
Colombia	65.53	41.19	0.63	1941
Peru	88.36	34.38	0.39	1953

1. Millions US$.
Source: Jorgenson and Sachs (1988).

Future Prospects for Debt Reduction

Besides general approaches to debt reduction, the outlook for debt repurchases and conversions by the public sector will depend on Chile's future export performance (especially copper prices) and on the government's budgetary situation. Regarding the latter one can say that Chile has been a model country and there are expectations that it will continue to be so.

For private sector repurchases, the size of private assets abroad is critical. By 1988 these assets were estimated at $3 billion (Larrain, 1988*b*). Other continuing sources of foreign exchange for these transactions are the parallel foreign exchange market, strongest in tourism, and under- and over-invoicing. Given the relatively small size of private debt in 1988, these resources, though falling, will continue to make a significant impact on private sector repurchases.

On the other hand, debt-equity swaps in the private sector will probably experience more and more social and political antagonism towards foreign ownership and may consequently slow. Debt-equity swaps in the public sector will be governed more by domestic political considerations.

Conclusion

Chile's external debt in 1982 was mostly private sector debt. In 1988, the situation was reversed: public sector debt had become the heavier of the two. Government's guarantees of much private sector debt (demanded by creditor banks) has helped transform the debt picture.

Chile has had substantial success in reducing interest rate spreads on its debt and extending maturities through renegotiations. In the other area of debt reduction (repurchases and conversions), Chile reduced its external commercial debt by $4.2 billion (from December 1984 to June 1988). Most reductions, about $3.2 billion, have been in private sector debt.

Chile's success is largely due to sound macro policies, especially the containment of domestic budgetary deficits and the consolidation of gains from economic restructuring. In addition, Chile's repurchase and conversion schemes have been well conceived and stable.

Debt reduction may be more difficult in the future for two reasons. First, much of the external debt is now concentrated in the public sector: repurchases and especially conversions are more difficult. Second, private sector debt has declined while private sector foreign exchange for these repurchases are more limited and assets for converting may be less available. Although Chile has not entirely solved its problems, it appears to have its external debt more under control than do other major Latin American debtors.

NOTES

1. *Source:* Central Bank of Chile.
2. After a while the government received a fee for this guarantee from the foreign banks – see French-Davis and De Gregorio (1985) and Larrain (1986).
3. For a discussion see Graces (1988).
4. The detailed regulation can be found in *Provision of The Conversion of External Debt,* Banco Central de Chile, Santiago, 1988.
5. This is avoided specifically when a debtor agrees to convert debt to the foreign entity into an equity investment is his or her firm or some other directly-owned assets. Similarly the government avoids borrowing or printing money if a public enterprise is privatised.
6. Bergsman and Edisis used interviews to analyse 104 of the 450 public debt-equity swaps in Argentina, Brazil, Chile and Mexico.
7. Bank acquisition of equity position in a non-financial institution is subject to regulation in most countries. In the U.S., for instance, up to mid 1987, banks had to keep their investment in any non-financial company below $15 million and 20 per cent of the voting stock and limited to five years. In February 1988 this regulation (Regulation K) was liberalised for investments in a large number of heavily indebted countries.
8. The figure for bank conversion is from June 1989, the others are from June 1988. We have therefore assumed that the percentage of bank conversions (i.e. 21.27 per cent) was the same as of June 1988. Thus, 21.27 per cent of all chapter XIX conversions were additional, while 78.73 per cent were 64 per cent additional, resulting in an overall additionality of 74.02 per cent.
9. Round tripping should be avoided in the screening process. In Chile case-by-case analysis of conversions, while relying on the financial records of the foreign company, is used to eliminate the likelihood of this most non-additional of all conversions.
10. There are clearly other differences, such as macro-economic management.
11. Central Bank of Chile.
12. Sachs' definition of debt reduction focuses on sub-market interest rates. These, however, may be hard to define. When rescheduling occurs at a rate below that available to countries for new money, this would appear to be sub-market interest rates. It is, however, not certain whether Sachs would consider this debt reduction.

Chapter 3

DEBT MANAGEMENT IN MEXICO

Introduction

Mexico's external debt began to grow rapidly in 1973, with most accumulation of foreign debt occurring in the five years between 1977 and 1982 (see Chapter 1). Most of Mexico's long-term debt in 1982 was contracted by its public sector. Since then, most of the increase in long-term debt is still attributable to the Mexican public sector. Meanwhile short-term lending to Mexico has fallen radically since 1982 largely because of the rescheduling of long-term debt and partly because of the termination of voluntary lending by commercial creditors.

External borrowing in 1973 by the public sector increased total public sector foreign debt from $5.5 billion in 1973 to $15.8 billion in 1976 and to $29 billion in 1979, and was used to finance the government's increasing fiscal deficit. During the period 1974-1979, foreign borrowing by the Mexican public sector financed around 60 per cent of the economic deficit. The government used this form of financing because the deficit's size made it difficult to finance by non-inflationary sources; worse domestic inflation had complicated financial intermediation; and before 1977 the government did not finance its deficit through the sale of bonds to the private sector.

Meanwhile, the contribution of commercial credit to Mexico's borrowing increased because of the increased size and value of Mexico's oil reserves. The expansion in public sector foreign debt from $29 billion in 1979 to nearly $60 billion by the end of 1982 was even more sudden than in the previous period. The borrowing was used to finance ambitious projects and capital flight by the private sector and government officials. As a result, the much-needed structural fiscal adjustment was postponed.

Mexico's external debt rose precipitously in the years leading up to 1982, but most of it was reflected in capital flight. When interest payments for previous borrowing are added to capital flight, Mexico received little in net resource transfer. Table 3.1 illustrates the partial decomposition of the increase in external debt (Buffie, 1988). Buffie's table indicates that the net resource transfer was never very large, while external indebtedness grew substantially. During the heaviest period of debt build-up (1977-1982), the non-interest current account deficit amounted to only 5 per cent of the increased indebtedness (last column, Table 3.1), and since 1982, net resource transfers to Mexico were negative. Moreover, the trend in capital flight has continued since 1982. Capital flight was induced by an overvalued exchange rate and low and negative real interest rates on domestic bank deposits for most of the period.

Since 1982 the composition of Mexico's external debt creditors has changed. In 1982, commercial creditors represented about 87 per cent of the outstanding credit to Mexico. By

Table 3.1. DEBT DECOMPOSITION

Billions of dollars

	1971-1976	1977-1982	1983-1986
Current Account Deficit			
Interest (A)[1]	6.00	31.63	34.98
Non-interest (B)	8.81	3.52	–44.60
Increase in debt (C)[2]	20.07	67.26	5.91
(B)/(C)	0.44	0.05	–

1. Private and public sector interest payments on the foreign debt plus remitted profits less income from Mexican investments abroad.
2. Net increase in private and public sector foreign debt plus net direct foreign investment.
Source: Buffie, 1988.

the end of 1988, their share was less than 80 per cent of a larger volume of debt. The change came at the end of voluntary lending to Mexico, with official creditors increasingly taking up the slack. Concurrently, the share of public sector (or guaranteed) debt in Mexico's total external indebtedness has grown. The shift is attributable to the following factors. First, the government nationalised private banks, effectively assuming their external debt. Second, the increasing portion of debt, official credit, was for the public sector. And third, debt reduction schemes have been proportionally used more by the private sector.

The focus of this chapter is an analysis of Mexico's debt management policies since 1982. The major components of these policies have been:

- rescheduling;
- debt-reduction schemes;
- hedging operations.

Rescheduling

Mexico began to take an active role in renegotiating its external debt in 1982. It used multi-year rescheduling agreements to extend repayments of principal, gain favourable repricing of interest rate margins on existing credits and interest rate margins on new credits, obtain new money to meet its external financial needs, and change the currency composition of its obligations.

By early 1982 it had become apparent to the Mexican authorities that their country could not honour its looming debt repayments in 1982 and beyond. In July, Mexico contacted the International Monetary Fund, hoping to reach an agreement, but no quick resolution emerged; Mexico was reluctant to make the necessary economic adjustments. On 23 August 1982 the country announced that it would suspend principal payments for the next 90 days. The banks formed an advisory committee and commenced discussions with Mexico, reaching an accord in December of that year.

Rescheduling improved Mexico's external profile in the following ways:

i) repayment and grace periods were lengthened at each renegotiation;

ii) reschedulings also applied to loans from 1982 on;

iii) the interest rate spreads over LIBOR and prime (eliminated as a bench-mark in 1986) declined from 2.25 per cent over LIBOR in 1982 to 0.8125 per cent;

iv) flat rescheduling and new money fees which were 1 per cent and 1.25 per cent of the face value in 1982 were reduced and eliminated; and

v) the currency composition of Mexican debt became somewhat more diversified.

The restructuring of external debt obligations and revisions of terms negotiated with major creditors since 1982 helped improve Mexico's external debt-service profile. Most of Mexico's short-term debt was converted into longer maturities in the restructuring exercise of 1982-1984. These obligations were again restructured as part of the multi-year rescheduling agreement reached in 1985 with the international banking community on amortization payments due during 1985-1990. The agreement, which also involved the rescheduling of principal obligations on the 1983 loan of $5 billion, covered approximately $48.7 billion of debt-service obligations. As part of the 1986/1987 financing package, and under great pressure from the U.S. government, there was a further restructuring of terms that postponed the first repayment on the 1983 loan until 1989 and deferred other repayments, extending the grace period to 1994. Meanwhile the interest rate spread was reduced to 13/16 of 1 per cent. Mexico's official creditors also restructured 100 per cent of the principal and 60 per cent of the interest due in the period from 22 September 1986 through 31 December 1987, as well as the principal maturing through the end of March 1988.

On 20 March 1987 the Mexican Government and Mexico's Commercial Bank creditors signed to implement the 1986/1987 financing package. In addition to the restructuring of a large share of Mexico's outstanding debt to banks, the agreement provided for new loans amounting to US$6 billion through March 1988, with contingent disbursements of an additional $1.7 billion in the event of a drop in oil prices or a failure of the economy to recover as projected. The loan would be reduced if oil prices reached levels higher than those projected. The first withdrawal under the arrangement ($3.5 billion) took place in April 1987. A second disbursement ($0.9 billion) was made in November 1987; this total amount was lowered by $128 million because oil prices in the first half of 1987 went up. Because of the favourable oil prices in 1987, $1.2 billion of contingent loans was no longer available, and the total new loan commitment of US$6 billion was reduced to $5.2 billion.

As part of the 1985 agreement with its creditors, Mexico offered non-U.S. banks the option of converting a part of their dollar-denominated debt into their own national currency. The conversion into non-dollar debt was to be gradual, with the phasing-in time dependent on the proportion of the debt a bank wanted to convert. The conversions were calculated at the prevailing market exchange rates.

Debt Reduction Schemes

Mexico has implemented two schemes to reduce its external debt – a debt-equity swap programme and a debt securitisation plan. The Brady Plan was awaiting ratification by banks in August 1989.

a) Debt-Equity Swap Programme

Mexico's debt-equity swap programme grew from the August 1985 agreement. Creditors had to waive certain clauses in syndicated loans (see Chapter 2 on Chile for a discussion of these) before Mexico could implement the programme. Under the agreement, Mexico could allow foreign investors to buy Mexican public debt and exchange it for equity in a public or private enterprise, complete an existing or initiate a new investment project, or prepay debts to Mexican banks (FICORCA – Foreign Exchange Risk Coverage Trust Fund; see below).

To acquire equity, the investor had to receive the approval of the Ministry of Finance, the Foreign Investment Board and the Ministry of Foreign Affairs. There were certain restrictions on the stock to be acquired. The equity had to be issued to foreign investors, non-convertible to true assets and non-transferable to a Mexican national for a period of over two years, and extraordinary dividends could not be received on it. At the same time, conversion could be made into other debt (instead of equity) or used to cancel peso debts, but required the authorisation of the Ministry of Finance and the Foreign Investment Board.

Initially, the swap programme was for Mexican nationals. Mexicans or Mexican entities could obtain public debt and convert the proceeds into approved domestic investment. However, when the actual regulations were published, these possibilities were scrapped. This is a major difference between the Mexican and Chilean programmes.

Most private sector debt was contracted by Mexican banks which acted as intermediaries for lending to the private sector in dollar-denominated loans. After the debt crisis and the devaluation of September 1982, Mexican firms could not service their dollar debts to the banks (which were nationalised that year). Consequently the government did not have the resources to service the Mexican commercial banks' debts or those directly incurred by the private sector. The FICORCA scheme was established later in 1982 to ameliorate this situation, and applied to any private sector dollar debt with a foreign or Mexican commercial bank[1]. The Mexican firm could reschedule its foreign debt to obtain a maturity of eight years or more and a grace period of at least four years. Then the firm could get a peso loan (at the official foreign exchange rate) equivalent to its amortization of principal from FICORCA to acquire dollars; this money would then be lent back to FICORCA. FICORCA would then service the dollar debt as long as the firm paid interest and principal payments on its peso debt.

In August 1987 the Mexican government agreed with commercial banks on a restructuring of private debt covered by the FICORCA scheme. When debt covered by the FICORCA scheme was repaid by the original private sector borrower, it would be assumed by the public sector and rescheduled on the same terms previously applied to the restructuring of the commercial bank debt of the public sector (i.e. 20 years' maturity with a grace period of seven years, and an interest rate spread of 13/16 per cent). Commercial banks would then have the option to re-lend the repaid amounts to local private sector borrowers at negotiated interest rates or leave the amount on deposit with the public sector. After the agreement many local private sector borrowers obtained very good discounts from their creditors for settlement of their outstanding obligations. A significant amount of such prepayments took place in late 1987; it should be noted that these were settlements, not prepayments – much of the debt payment was long overdue.

In essence the Mexican debt scheme was intended for the foreign investor to implement debt-equity swaps or prepay peso debts at a deep discount. Only later, after

August 1987, did it allow Mexicans to repurchase external debt, and the Mexican programme did not include conversions by the private sector into domestic assets.

In any case, the debt-equity swaps programme in Mexico was cancelled in October, 1987. The main reason was its adverse effect on domestic money supply and, hence, on inflation.

b) The Mexican Bond Scheme

We described in detail in Chapter 1 the difficulties encountered in the bond scheme proposed by the Morgan Guaranty Trust and the Mexican government. Perhaps it would have been more successful if commercial creditors had believed that Mexico was creditworthy and not looking for "debt forgiveness", but the value of the bonds was very hard to assess.

Another problem with the bond scheme was that, to be successful, both creditors and debtors would have to gain. Both sides might have benefited from a purchase of Mexican debt if the Mexican value on the debt was higher than the bank's (so if these values overlapped, the room for negotiation would increase). However, the overlapping of the value put on the outstanding Mexican paper by banks and by Mexico, as revealed in its bond offer, left very little room for negotiation. A third party could have made up some of the difference to both parties, but none was willing.

In the wake of the Mexico-Morgan plan, variations have been proposed to widen its scope and make it more appealing to creditors. First, many Third World countries do not have the necessary foreign exchange to buy zero-coupon collateral. Third parties (like international institutions or governments) could contribute grants or loans to the initial down-payment. Second, because of the importance of interest payments relative to the principal component of the new bonds, the scheme's attractiveness to creditors would be enhanced by third party guarantees of interest; interest insurance; creditor agreement (100 per cent consent) to allow Mexico to treat these bonds *de jure* senior to other Mexican debt (bonds have *de facto* been treated as senior). An insured interest payment stream (or guarantee for a minimum interest stream) within a loan/bond swap scheme (e.g. the Mexico-Morgan Plan) would probably result in a lower market discount rate for the anticipated stream of coupon payments.

c) The Brady Plan

The 23 July 1989 debt accord between Mexico and its creditor banks was the first application of the Brady Plan. The agreement allows Mexico to obtain debt relief through three options available to participating commercial banks:

1. exchange the old loans for 30-year bonds at a 35 per cent discount to face value while the interest remains the same rate as for old loans (13/16 per cent over LIBOR) – this essentially calls for a reduction of the principal by 35 per cent; or
2. exchange the old loans for 30-year bonds with par value and a fixed interest rate of 6.25 per cent (this lowers the interest rate to 6.25 per cent); or
3. provide new financing (or recycle interest received from Mexico) for four years. Under this option, the banks would have to commit an equivalent of 25 per cent of their present-day medium- and long-term exposure.

Banks opting for the bonds will have their interest payments guaranteed for at least eighteen months by the IMF, World Bank, Mexico and Japan; beyond eighteen months the length of this guarantee will depend on the number of banks providing new money. The bonds' principal would be guaranteed by a zero-coupon Treasury Bond.

Alan Greenspan, Chairman of the U.S. Federal Reserve, announced that after conducting a bank-by-bank analysis, approximately one-fifth have chosen to exchange loans at a 35 per cent discount for 30-year U.S. Treasury zero-coupon bonds. This in effect provides Mexico with US$2.35 billion in new financing for four years. About 60 per cent of other banks involved have opted to exchange loans for par value, paying only 6.25 per cent. The Mexican government has expressed its concern that these findings may show that the agreement ends up saving Mexico only US$1.2 billion a year (depending on which options the banks choose), and that it would have preferred to see more than just one-fifth of the 530 banks involved choosing a reduction in principal.

The Mexican government has planned to cut the net transfer of resources from the current 6 per cent of GDP to 2 per cent. The 6 per cent calculation is based on the average net transfer of resources over a six-year period from 1983 to 1988. The new accord of the fifteen-bank steering committee mandates that approximately US$15 billion of Mexico's debt to commercial banks be waived. Of this US$15 billion, 30 per cent would be absorbed by U.S. banks and the rest by European and Japanese banks.

However, as the 530 bank creditors have yet (as of August, 1989) to reach an agreement among themselves, the question remains – how many creditor banks will reject the agreement. Some may insist that Mexico honour its financial obligations.

It is easy to be pessimistic about Secretary Brady's Plan – there seems to be no long-term benefit for participating banks. Although the plan will ease the annual debt-service payments, it may not restore Mexico's ability to service new debt. The best scenario keeps Mexico's foreign debt from increasing over the next four years, hardly an incentive for the debtor banks. The problem is partly that the "multilateral agencies" have not come up with enough incentives for banks to opt for the new bonds. These agencies are reluctant to provide the guaranteed money up front; instead they will allocate the cash, from 1990 onwards, in stages. Japan has followed the lead of the IMF and World Bank and also plans to stagger its US$2 billion support.

There is also a vast difference of opinion among the 530 creditor banks on Mexico's prospects. Some banks hesitate to swap their loans at a discount; they believe that Mexico might overcome its foreign debt. However, as interest rates have fallen from 11.3 per cent to 9.5 per cent, some banks are more willing to swap their loans for the 6.25 per cent coupon bonds. While the majority of U.S. banks have enough reserves against their debt to absorb the 35 per cent discount, others might camouflage their losses under FASB 15 – an accounting standard that would categorise Mexican bonds as "trouble restructuring" and would allow the banks to bypass any new provisions.

Moreover, the banks managed to negotiate for a debt-equity swap. In the context of the Brady Plan negotiations, this was one of the main points of contention. This package, though limited due to its numerous restrictions, will permit an annual US$1 billion in debt-equity transactions over a period of three and a half years. However, it is important to point out that this "recapture clause" would be useless if oil prices drop; i.e. interest rates will not ease.

This plan is under furious attack from banks that do not want to offer new financing or swap their loans, but opt for collecting the interest due from Mexico. These banks would be placed *de facto* at the bottom of the list for debt-service receipts, hence, their loans would be the last to be serviced. Some of these banks have threatened legal action, as they are, in essence, being forced to comply with the plan.

This accord is unlikely to result in a solution to Mexico's debt problem; it may be only a temporary relief, depending on the choices the banks make among the options offered – or not offered. Rescheduling and debt relief can alleviate Third World debt problems, but only if the economy is not mismanaged (overvalued exchange rates, high inflation, negative real interest rates, etc.), because this inevitably leads to capital flight – the core of Mexico's historic economic problem.

Hedging Operations

The only public scheme focuses on currency diversification of debt at the option of non-U.S. creditor banks. The rules are as follows:

- If 30 per cent or less of a creditor's loan is targeted for re-denomination into its domestic currency, then the change in denomination would be carried out on an equal monthly basis (at the prevailing exchange rate) over a two-year period.
- For 40 per cent to 30 per cent, the process is the same but over two and a half years.
- For 50 per cent to 40 per cent, the process is again the same but the period is increased to three and a half years.
- A maximum of 50 per cent of debt can be converted.

Around $12 billion of the total Mexican debt was made eligible for conversion into other currencies. It is estimated that only $4 billion has been converted to date.

Impact of Conversions and Bond Schemes on the Size of Mexican Debt

From its operation in June 1986 to November 1987, when the programme was temporarily suspended, 404 applications from foreign investors were considered by the Mexican government. The face value of the amount of debt converted, approved and pending as of April 1988 is shown in Table 3.2. Of these conversions, roughly 75 per cent were foreign investment projects (i.e. FDI) by June 1987, while the other 25 per cent paid peso debts to Mexican banks or FICORCA[2].

Table 3.2. CONVERSIONS BY FOREIGN INVESTMENTS

Status	Number of Projects	Face Value ($ million)
Converted	299	2 974
Approved (not disbursed)	26	181
Approved (pending)	60	337
Pending Approval	19	111

Source: Hacienda, adapted from Sangines (1989).

Although no formal mechanism exists, applications of Mexican investors for conversion were also accepted after March 1987[3]. By November 1987, 32 such applications had been received; four had been authorised with a face value of $34 million; and 28 are pending, with a face value of $2 770 million.

In the case of the Mexican bond scheme, the face value of debt reduction amounted to $3.67 billion, while $2.56 billion in new Mexican bonds were issued. This resulted in a debt reduction of $1.11 billion. Mexico also allocated $532 million of foreign exchange to acquire the U.S. zero coupon bonds, resulting in a net debt reduction of only $578 million.

The results of the conversion and bond schemes can be summarised as follows:

i) Debt reduction through conversion (by foreign investors) made a modest contribution to reducing Mexican debt ($2 974 billion).

ii) The contribution of the Mexican bond scheme on a net face value basis was a modest $578 million, even less on a present discounted basis.

iii) The contribution of Mexican investors in conversions has been a paltry $34 million.

iv) In view of the heavy application for conversion by Mexican nationals, approval still pending, this appears to be a potentially large source of debt reduction (from flight capital).

Issues Raised by Debt Reduction Schemes

Mexico's debt reduction schemes, while contributing a much lower percentage than Chile's to cut commercial debt, raise similar issues of domestic macro-economic management; benefits to Mexico *versus* investors; additionality of conversions; future potential; and sufficient debt reduction.

Macro-economic Management and Debt Reduction

As mentioned in the case of Chile, debt conversion has important domestic financial implications. A private sector debtor would have to borrow pesos or use liquid peso assets to fund the conversion[4], and in the case of public debt, the Central Bank could expand the money supply, causing inflation, or borrow in the domestic market, raising interest rates. These are avoided if the object of the conversion is the sale of a public enterprise – i.e. to finance privatisation. Mexico's privatisation from swaps has entailed transactions with a face value of $4 million, an insignificant figure.

The purchase (instead of conversion) of a country's debt requires foreign exchange unless it is from final sellers in local currency. Official exchange reserves, private sector assets abroad, and the parallel market are the three possibilities. The parallel market increases the demand for foreign exchange and depreciates the peso. Mexico, unlike Chile, has not had a debt repurchase programme for the private sector. The public sector's major programme was the rather small Mexican bond scheme. These debt repurchase transactions have not, therefore, caused macro-economic management difficulties for Mexico. The conversion schemes, on the other hand, have.

The two types of conversions in Mexico – equity swaps and payment of debts to banks, or FICORCA – have had vastly different effects on domestic economic management. To finance the debt-equity swaps, the government (which, due to postponing needed structural adjustment) had only one choice. It did not have the foreign exchange to buy pesos, and the Mexican debt market is not as developed as that of Chile, so the government could not borrow domestically. The Ministry of Finance had to resort to borrowing from the Central Bank, directly increasing the monetary base. In the case of debt repayments or FICORCA, at the moment of the transaction there were no immediate effects on the money supply. When debt-servicing for FICORCA becomes due, however, the money supply will have to be expanded.

Measuring the impact of swaps on inflation in 1987 is beyond the scope of this study. However, some limited observations can be made[5]. The monetary base increased 37.2 per cent between January and September of 1987 (in October the swap programme was suspended). Roughly one-third of this increase was directly linked to the programme. The impact of the increase of the monetary base on inflation came on top of the government's large fiscal deficit and the 30 per cent devaluation of the peso. All these factors contributed to a high rate of inflation in 1987 (see Table 3.3). As Sangines (1989) has noted:

> "Hence, to sustain the mounting fiscal deficit a drop in the real monetary base would have to be compensated for by an explosively large increase in the inflation rate. The accumulation of international reserves and the prepayment of external debt through the swap program were paid for dearly. The expansion of the money supply gave rise to such a high inflation rate that the total revenues from the inflation tax started to fall. The marginal effect of the swaps on the money supply was particularly severe at such a critical level of inflation."

The Mexican experience shows that the macro-economic liability of debt reduction schemes are greatly determined by general economic conditions. If the government's domestic budget is balanced, it is easier to accommodate conversions, and if domestic capital markets are developed, the menu of choices eases the inflationary impact. When compared to the Chilean experience, debt repurchases by the private sector may be easier to absorb, especially because in Mexico a large pool of flight capital exists.

Table 3.3. MONTHLY RATE OF INFLATION 1987

Per cent

	Rate
January	8.1
February	7.2
March	6.6
April	8.7
May	7.5
June	7.2
July	8.1
August	8.2
September	7.5

Source: Central Bank of Mexico (Sangines, 1989).

The Accrual of Benefits of Debt Discount

As mentioned, the two channels for using swaps to reduce external debt in Mexico are: conversion of public debt for equity in a state enterprise, and conversion of public debt for investment in Mexico, or to pay a debt to a Mexican bank or FICORCA.

To implement a conversion, the foreign investor applies to the Ministry of Finance and includes his financial statement for the past three years, the amount and source of public debt acquired and the proposed target of the conversion. The Ministry of Finance authorises the conversion, but also negotiates the discount at which it would convert the public debt into pesos for investment or debt repayment in Mexico. The procedures were not "open", however, as they were in Chile; the process was complicated and cumbersome, and often based on factors like personal relations instead of market mechanisms.

In Mexico the discount at conversion was negotiated administratively instead of determined by auction. In Chile the discount was negotiated for foreign investors but was auctioned for Chilean nationals' repurchase of Chilean debt. As we have seen, the relative amounts of the available discount that accrue to the country and the foreign investor are important in assessing the benefits of conversion schemes.

In Mexico the range of negotiated discounts has varied between 0 and 25 per cent[6]. More favourable terms have been offered for:

- companies to be privatised;
- high technology areas;
- projects generating foreign exchange;
- labour-intensive projects;
- small and middle-size businesses;
- companies with 100 per cent foreign ownership.

Table 3.4. DISCOUNTS BY SECTORS

	Average Discount	Number of Deals
Automobiles	11.74	15
Tourism	10.42	47
In-bond Assembly Plants	10.08	35
Metallic Products	11.00	13
Chemicals	13.09	20
Manufacturing	12.83	22
Metal Foundries	14.20	7
Services (Health Care)	8.00	1
Agro-businesses	14.40	10
Textiles and Leather Goods	12.82	4
Electronics	12.22	12
Mining	13.02	4
Construction	12.50	6
Others	9.45	11

Source: Secretaria de Hacienda (Sangines, 1989).

The size of the discount varied according to the attributes of the proposed investment. By sector of investment, the size of discount varied from 8 per cent to 14.4 per cent (see Table 3.4).

The average discount on Mexican debt on the secondary market was 45 per cent. Of this discount, Mexico captured on average one-third.

Additionality

The question of additionality does not apply to the net debt reduction in the Mexican bond scheme, since it did not result in any direct foreign investment. Thus additionality covers $2.97 billion of conversions by foreign investors. Bank investment in Mexico would probably not have occurred unless Mexican debt was selling at a discount and a programme was in place. The size of a bank's conversions for its own portfolio is not known. However, a conversion resulted from the debt capitalisation of the reorganisation of the Mexican company Groupo Alfa. Here the creditor banks traded $920 million in Groupo Alfa debt for a 45 per cent equity interest plus $25 million in currency and $200 million in Mexican government debt. In this way $720 million in debt was retired in 1986. This was not a conversion in the normal sense because the creditor banks took large losses when faced with Alfa's bankruptcy.

Of the $2 974 million in conversions, roughly 25 per cent were for debt repayment, leaving $2 230 million of debt-equity swaps. If we further assume that the Groupo Alfa conversions were all additional, as they were acquired by commercial creditors, this leaves $1 510 million in conversions open to the question of additionality – the amount of the conversions by foreign private investors and multinational corporations. Bergsman and Edisis' (1988) interviews with multinational corporation investors in Mexico have led them to conclude that 44 per cent of these conversions were additional. Thus $830 million of the total Mexican conversion may be considered non-additional.

Sangines' (1989) rough analysis also supports the view of substantial additionality. He notes that total direct foreign investment increased by 185 per cent between 1985 and 1986

Table 3.5. FOREIGN DIRECT INVESTMENT

$ billion

	FDI
1970	200.7
1975	295.7
1978	385.1
1982	708.7
1983	373.8
1984	391.1
1985	490.5
1986	905.5
1987[1]	1 418.7

1. January-September
Source: Banco de Mexico (Sangines, 1989).

(see Table 3.5); 50 per cent during 1986/1987 was swap-financed. This rise may have been partly motivated by the steep devaluation of the peso, leaving the issue open to question.

Future Prospects for Debt Reduction

The outlook for debt repurchases and conversions by the public sector will depend on Mexico's future export performance (especially oil prices), on the government's budget (which suffers from severe problems), and on the design and continuity of Mexico's conversion programme. The medium-term outlook for oil prices is not optimistic because of the excess production capacity in OPEC countries. As for Mexico's conversion programme, its design could be changed in several ways:

i) formally include Mexican nationals into the conversion and repurchase scheme, as in Chile;
ii) use auctions to capture more of the discount;
iii) borrow rather than print money to finance conversions; the most beneficial policy will keep government finances under control and reduce inflation;
iv) attain continuity in the programme.

Finally, the Brady Plan may make a valuable contribution to Mexico's debt problem.

NOTES

1. This excluded the foreign debt of Mexican commercial banks which were already nationalised.
2. Sangines, 1989.
3. *op. cit.*
4. This is avoided specifically when a debtor agrees to convert his debt to the foreign entity into an equity investment in his firm or some other assets that he directly owns.
5. Sangines, 1989.
6. *op. cit.*

Chapter 4

SUFFICIENT DEBT RELIEF

Introduction

As we have seen, debt-related difficulties have probably slowed investment and growth in some heavily indebted countries. This effect, commonly referred to as "debt overhang", acts like a tax on current and future income, and results in a large proportion of income growth accruing to foreigners. A reduction in debt-servicing during periods of financial difficulty would help maintain investment, as high debt service payments reduce the return to investment and hence adversely affect its level. This was demonstrated in 1982 in the flow of external financing that forced debtor countries to adjust their external current account balances. Their investment performance was poor compared to that of other developing countries. This led to the presumption that debt-servicing, investment and growth are related, and that sufficient reduction in debt-servicing could break the vicious debt trap and encourage higher investment and growth.

Growth in developing countries since 1982 has been considerably weaker than in the previous six-year period, especially among the fifteen heavily indebted countries. Chile had a GDP growth rate of around 8 per cent during the period 1976-1981, falling to 4 per cent from 1982 to 1988. This decline was also apparent in investment/GDP ratios. Chile's ratio fell from around 17 per cent in the period 1976-1981 to around 13 per cent in the period 1982-1988. Mexico's annual GDP growth rate declined from 9.5 per cent during 1976-1981 to around 0 per cent during 1982-1988; while its investment/GDP ratio fell from around 24 per cent to 19 per cent over the same period.

Sufficient Debt Relief

Sufficient debt relief that would permit a country to service its remaining debt while its economy grows at a satisfactory rate could improve creditworthiness and access to commercial financing. On the other hand, some forms of debt relief could cause creditors' disengagement. Depending on how debt relief is achieved, potential benefit to creditors may also increase the net present value of commercial loans to developing countries (see below).

Sufficient debt relief as defined above is certainly not an easy task. It depends on external conditions like the demand for a country's exports, which naturally affects their value; terms of trade, which affect real income; the level of interest rates on its external borrowing, which affects its debt-servicing burden, etc. It also depends on domestic developments beyond its control; weather or political developments, for example. Above all it depends on domestic policies. Devising a model that would include all the above is beyond

Table 4.1a. CHILE: REQUIRED INVESTMENT RATE PLUS DEBT-SERVICING

As a percentage of GDP

Assumed *Per Capita* Growth Rate	3.0	3.5	4.0
Projected Population Growth Rate	1.2	1.2	1.2
Assumed Growth Rate	4.2	4.7	5.2
Corresponding Required Investment Rate[1]	15.96	17.86	19.76
Projected Debt-Servicing to GDP[2]	8.42	8.31	8.21
Corresponding Required Investment Rate Plus Projected External Debt-Servicing	24.38	26.17	27.97

1. Marginal Capital – Output Ratio = 3.8 (average for 1973-1988).
2. Projected average for 1988-1992.

the scope of this study. A simple approximate concept is, however, available. Using the Harrod-Domar approach:

$$I = S = nv$$

where
- I = investment rate
- S = savings rate
- n = natural growth rate (population)
- v = marginal capital - output ratio

We could assume different adequate rates of *per capita* growth – 3.0 per cent, 3.5 per cent and 4 per cent. Taking the expected (1986-2000, World Bank, 1988) rate of growth of population for Chile of 1.2 per cent per annum, adequate overall growth rates become 4.2 per cent, 4.7 per cent and 5.2 per cent; for Mexico, given an expected population growth of 2.1 per cent, the adequate overall growth becomes 5.15, 5.6 per cent and 6.1 per cent. With a marginal capital-output ratio of 3.8 (average over the period 1973-1980) for Chile, and 3.3 for Mexico, we calculate the necessary levels of investment in Tables 4.1a and 4.1b. In Tables 4.2a and 4.2b the required investment plus debt-servicing at different assumed growth rates is compared to the various gross savings rates, while required investment rate is compared to national savings rate, to determine the projected shortfall in domestic

Table 4.1b. MEXICO: REQUIRED INVESTMENT RATE PLUS PROJECTED DEBT-SERVICING

As a percentage of GDP

Assumed *Per Capita* Growth Rate	3.0	3.5	4.0
Projected Population Growth Rate	2.1	2.1	2.1
Assumed Growth Rate	5.1	5.6	6.1
Corresponding Required Investment Rate[1]	16.83	18.48	20.13
Projected Debt-Servicing to GDP[2]	8.1	8.05	8.0
Corresponding Required Investment Rate Plus Projected External Debt-Servicing	24.93	26.53	28.13

1. Marginal Capital – Output Ratio = 3.3 (average for 1973-1988).
2. Projected average for 1988-1992.

Table 4.2a. CHILE: PROJECTED EXCESS SAVINGS/GDP

In percentages

Assumed Growth Rate	4.2	4.7	5.2
Corresponding Required Investment Plus Projected Debt-Servicing Rate	24.38	26.17	27.97
Projected Gross Domestic Savings Rate of 23.30%[1]	–1.08	–2.87	–4.67
Corresponding Required Investment Rate	15.6	17.86	19.67
Projected National Savings Rate of 15.20%[1]	–0.40	–2.66	–4.47

1. High for 1985-1988.

savings. Finally, in Tables 4.3a and 4.3b is calculated the implied percentage reduction in debt-servicing to achieve various growth rates.

We should note in interpreting these results that the difference between gross and national savings rates is factor payments (largely debt-service). Thus, in using gross savings figures to determine debt-service reduction, the comparison is to required investment plus projected debt-service obligation; and in the case of national savings, it is to required investment.

The results for Chile (Table 4.3a) show that Chile requires roughly 10 per cent debt-service relief to grow at 4.2 per cent (3.0 per cent *per capita*) while servicing its remaining debt; the corresponding figures are roughly 33 per cent reduction to grow at 4.7 per cent and a 55 per cent reduction to grow at 5.2 per cent.

Table 4.3b shows that Mexico has in fact enough savings to grow at 5.2 per cent (3 per cent *per capita*) and 5.7 per cent; it is only at the 6.2 per cent rate of growth that savings inadequacies require debt-service reduction. These results, however, mask one important fact – capital flight. In Chile, this has not been a significant issue, especially in recent years, but in Mexico, capital flight has been one of the most unfortunate byproducts of the Mexican economy (see Chapter 1). In Table 4.3c, the results of Table 4.3b are reproduced with an allowance for historical rates (1982-1987 average) of capital flight of 6.9 per cent of GDP. These results compared to debt reduction without capital flight demonstrate Mexico's dilemma. If debt reduction stimulates better policies and confidence in the economy, thus

Table 4.2b. MEXICO: PROJECTED EXCESS SAVINGS/GDP

In percentages

Assumed Growth Rate	5.1	5.6	6.1
Corresponding required Investment Plus Projected Debt Servicing Rate	24.93	26.53	28.13
Projected Gross Domestic Savings Rate of 25.80%[1]	+0.87	+0.73	–2.33
Corresponding required Investment Rate	16.83	18.48	20.13
Projected National Savings Rate of 20.30%[1]	+3.47	+1.82	+0.17

1. High for 1985-1988.

Table 4.3a. CHILE: FINANCING GAP:
REQUIRED DEBT-SERVICING REDUCTION

In percentages of projected debt-servicing[1]

		Gross	National
Projected Savings Rate		23.30	15.20
Assumed Growth	4.2		
Required Debt-Servicing Reduction		–12.8	–4.8
Assumed Growth	4.7		
Required Debt-Servicing Reduction		–34.5	–32.0
Assumed Growth	5.2		
Required Debt-Servicing Reduction		–56.9	–54.4

1. [–] denotes debt reduction.

ending capital flight, Mexico needs no debt-service reduction. If it does not, debt-service reductions would have to be so large as to be unrealistic. So Mexico is caught in a classic trap. In fact, if debt reduction induces better policies and capital flight is reversed, resulting in large reverse inflows of capital, Mexico's future will be much brighter than even the results of Table 4.3b indicate.

An issue raised by this approach is the constraints of foreign exchange. A country may have enough savings to grow at a certain rate, but foreign exchange availability may still limit its growth. In most of the heavily indebted countries, however, savings appear to be the binding restriction to growth, so that foreign exchange limitations may not be crucial. Another shortcoming is that the marginal capital-output ratio is an average, and the impact of investment on growth will depend on the particular sector of investment.

At the same time, historic savings rates have been used in these projections; in fact, we have used the highest levels of the last five years. Using the highest levels may appear too

Table 4.3b. MEXICO: FINANCING GAP:
REQUIRED DEBT-SERVICING REDUCTION

In percentages of projected debt-servicing[1]

		Gross	National
Projected Savings Rate		25.80	20.30
Assumed Growth	5.1		
Required Debt-servicing Reduction		10.7	42.8
Assumed Growth	5.6		
Required Debt-servicing Reduction		9.1	22.6
Assumed Growth	6.1		
Required Debt-servicing Reduction		–29.1	2.1

1. [–] denotes debt reduction.

Table 4.3c. MEXICO: FINANCING GAP: REQUIRED DEBT-SERVICING REDUCTION WHILST ACCOUNTING FOR CAPITAL FLIGHT

In percentages of projected debt-servicing[1]

		Gross	National
Projected Savings Rate		25.80	20.30
Assumed Growth	5.1		
Required Debt-servicing Reduction		–74.4	–42.3
Assumed Growth	5.6		
Required Debt-servicing Reduction		–76.6	–63.3
Assumed Growth	6.1		
Required Debt-servicing Reduction		–115.4	–84.1

1. [–] denotes debt reduction.

optimistic, but improved economic confidence may induce higher savings rates than those of the 1980s and could surpass those projected. Finally, other mechanisms of debt relief like debt-equity swaps and debt reschedulings may reduce projected debt-service, calling for less debt-service reductions; we have endeavoured to incorporate this effect into the projections. In any case the results should be viewed as an approximation of the magnitude of sufficient debt reduction.

Conclusion

Although these rough calculations are only a guess at the levels of debt-service reduction that may be required, more sophisticated calculations will probably not diminish the amount of sufficient debt reduction. The point, however, is that debt reduction schemes will probably not solve the debt crisis once and for all unless sufficient debt relief is at hand. Even then one must hope for incentives that will improve country policies so that growth and the ability to service debt are enhanced.

FUTURE PROSPECTS

The Debt Picture

During the 1970s and early 1980s many developing countries borrowed heavily on commercial terms. Unfortunately their domestic policies were not structured to take advantage of the massive inflow of resources. Worse, domestic investment ratios did not rise to reflect the higher level of resource availability; this was a precursor of the debt crisis. The inflow of resources was used instead mainly to finance consumption and flight capital.

Adverse external economic developments and the reluctance of commercial banks to maintain what are in retrospect unsustainable levels of lending led to the debt crisis. It has gone through various phases – the inability of Mexico and other heavily indebted countries to service their debt, their open-ended financial and economic difficulties and loss of creditworthiness and access to commercial credit, and deteriorating balance sheets and income statements of commercial banks. There have been proposals of partial measures to solve the immediate problem. Short-term loans (from the IMF / World Bank / BIS), financial support from OECD governments, reduced commercial financing and debt-service postponement (through formal debt renegotiations) were the initial responses. They were followed by attempts to improve the commercial banks' financial situation and support for market-based mechanisms (the menu approach). The menu approach included favourable multi-year debt renegotiations, debt-for-equity swaps, debt for bond exchange, debt buybacks and interest capitalisation. These measures, though salutary, have not culminated in a restoration of creditworthiness to heavily indebted countries.

The traditional approach has neglected the core of the debt crisis, namely that the current level of contractual debt-service is so high that resumption of contractual debt service payments and domestic economic growth are inconsistent, especially since debtors have few incentives to make the tremendous sacrifice involved in re-ordering domestic policies. At the same time, creditors have not been motivated to unilaterally reduce debt-service payments or income losses that do not raise the value of their portfolios. This has resulted in a debt trap. The Brady Plan was conceived in such a context – through debt-service reductions – to break the debt trap and improve economic and financial conditions for debtors as well as creditors.

The Chilean and Mexican Experience

Chile and Mexico accumulated substantial external debt during the period 1975-1987. This accumulation was not accompanied by a commensurate increase in investment. Adverse external developments and domestic policy inconsistencies have made the period after 1982 difficult. The ratio of investment to GDP in the post-1982 period has been lower than that of preceding years; growth, too, has been lower. However, these conditions were less pronounced in Chile than in Mexico.

Chile's main domestic policy failures have been the backward indexation of wages coupled with the fixed exchange rates initiated in 1979. This has caused a substantial real appreciation of the peso resulting in loss of export competitiveness and, in the absence of capital controls, heavy external borrowing by the private sector. The policy began to be reversed in 1982 but it has taken time. In 1985 Chile strove for a real depreciation of the peso, export stimulation and diversification, and a more favourable current account picture. During most of this time the government's fiscal condition was good, especially compared to other problem debtors like Mexico. Mexico embarked in 1971 on a tremendous fiscal expansion, temporarily reversed in 1977. After the oil euphoria of 1978, the fiscal expansion started again. The immediate result of this deficit spending policy was accelerated inflation. Coupled with interest rate controls and a pegged peso it spurred negative real interest rates and a decline in real exchange rates. This discouraged investment and promoted imports and capital flight.

The major differences between Chilean and Mexican policies have been Chile's ability to control public finances, giving policy makers more room for manœvre; and its policy of adopting better economic policies earlier and sticking with them, thus consolidating achievements and renewing public confidence in the domestic economy.

Both Chile and Mexico have received assistance from successful debt renegotiations in the area of debt management. Specifically, the terms of commercial debt, repayment and grace periods have been lengthened at each renegotiation; renegotiation has also applied to loans since 1983; the interest rate spreads over LIBOR or prime have declined sharply; flat one-time rescheduling and new money fees have been reduced, even eliminated; the frequency of interest payments has been slowed; and finally, benefits have accrued from lower cost for co-financing loans.

In addition to debt renegotiation, Chile was the first debtor country to establish a workable regulatory framework for debt reduction. Amendments and waivers by creditor banks enabled Chile to set up two main formal channels to accommodate the swapping of its medium- and long-term debt – chapter XVIII conversions that accommodate debt conversions by Chilean nationals and Chapter XIX for foreign investors.

The impact of these and other debt reduction schemes has been powerful. At 1 June 1988, total private and public debt reduction stood at US$4 192.4 million, while commercial debt was $11 834.1 million and total debt was $16 512.9 million.

Mexico also established two debt reduction schemes: the debt-equity swap programme and a debt securitisation plan (the Mexico-Morgan Plan). The first enabled foreign investors to buy public Mexican debt to swap for equity in a public or private enterprise, complete an existing or initiate a new investment project, or prepay debts to Mexican banks (FICORCA). The programme did not allow its own nationals to convert foreign debt into domestic assets. The Mexico-Morgan plan allowed commercial bank creditors to exchange Mexican loans for new Mexican government bonds at higher rates of interest. The principal was collateralised by U.S. Government zero-coupon bonds bought by Mexico.

Today, in light of Mexican total debt over US$100 billion, the effect of the debt reduction schemes on Mexico's total indebtedness is not overwhelming. It is estimated that debt conversion reduced Mexican debt by only $4.2 billion. The bond scheme reduced total debt by $578 million and contributions by Mexican investors resulted in a conversion of only US$34 million. There are a large number of applications still pending from Mexican investors, however, representing a sizeable potential reduction in debt. In addition, conversions from Mexican nationals would recapture flight capital from abroad.

Chilean debt reduction programmes have been more successful. Nevertheless, while Chile's debt reduction programmes have undoubtedly helped reduce commercial debt, several important issues applying both to Chile and Mexico have been raised in the process. These are problems of domestic macro-economic management, benefits to Chile and Mexico versus investors, additionality of conversions, future potential and efficient debt reduction.

Between January and September of 1987, the monetary base in Mexico increased 37.2 per cent. It is estimated that approximately one-third of this increase was an outcome of the swap programme. With the devaluation of the peso and the high fiscal deficit, this stimulated high rates of inflation, forcing the cancellation of the Mexican programme in October 1987.

Without sound macro-economic policies the impact of debt conversion programmes is questionable (in the absence of good policies, everything is questionable). Except for the sale of public entities through a conversion programme, Mexico could obtain superior results by limiting conversions to the private sector. Inasmuch as the public sector increases interest rates by taxing the domestic capital markets (if domestic capital is available) to execute conversions, private sector conversions would access flight capital. Its repatriation would not only supply an infusion of needed funds, but persuade the investor to have a stake in the domestic economy.

In both Chile and Mexico, additionality appears to have been high. While conversions in Chile have been important in reducing commercial debt, conversions cannot be viewed as a solution. Conversions require good domestic policies, confidence in the local economy and desirable investment opportunities. The latter could become a possible political problem and thus a limiting factor, even in Chile, if a large share of high-profile assets were held by foreigners; again this problem has been somewhat ameliorated in Chile due to large conversions by Chilean nationals.

Whither from here?

Many debtors require some relief to be able to restore economic growth, but any realistic debt scheme must simultaneously render both debtors and creditors better off than they were before the plan. Unfortunately, if a plan features a pie that must only be divided, then it is a zero sum game. To succeed, a scheme must create a larger pie. The problem is how to increase it. There are several possibilities:

a) Financial contribution by third parties such as OECD governments; this could take many forms, including the purchase of Third World debt and debt forgiveness. This option is more or less unrealistic.

b) Leveraged financial contribution by third parties in the form of debt-service guarantees for newly reconstituted margin debt.

c) Improved economic and financial policies in debtor countries through better adjustment incentives. This may involve some form of conditional debt-service reduction or debt relief. Here debt servicing would be indexed to a country's debt-servicing capacity outside the country's control, such as an index of prices of its major exports. When debt-servicing capacity falls, a proportion of contractual debt-servicing could be capitalised and *vice versa.*

d) Favourable changes in accounting and tax treatment of Third World loans in major creditor countries to improve the financial position of commercial banks; this would have to be based on corresponding debt forgiveness and relief by commercial creditors.

For such an approach to work, debt relief must be sufficient. The traditional market-oriented approach, though beneficial to some, is unlikely to provide sufficient debt relief for most countries. Debt buy-backs and debt securitisation will probably not succeed without third party support. Although buy-backs and securitisation have identical impacts on debt (or debt-service) reduction, they present different problems. Debt buy-backs are by definition not an option for countries with little or no reserves. Effective debt securitisation is unworkable unless third party guarantees are forthcoming. Both also present different problems in the form of debt seniority and tax and accounting treatment in creditor-debtor relations. Debt-equity swaps, too, though useful, are limited in reducing debt, especially in countries which are already experiencing serious macro-economic difficulties (such as budget problems).

The Brady Plan proposes solutions along the lines of our recommendations. Its application in the case of Mexico, however, points to several deficiencies.

i) Commercial debt should be reduced through a negotiated discount that induces all banks to participate and keeps banks engaged. Unfortunately it appears that some banks may not go along with the agreement in Mexico's case. This could result in non-participating banks seizing Mexican assets since the new securities to be issued will be treated as senior to loans. Under these circumstances it is unlikely that banks remain engaged in Mexican lending.

ii) It is not sure, even if all banks participate, that the debt-servicing reduction will be sufficient to restore growth and enable Mexico to service its newly restructured debt.

iii) Advantageous revisions in tax and accounting treatment would have helped the plan – they could have motivated all banks to participate.

iv) Another positive feature would have been a more comprehensive conditional debt-servicing feature for newly structured debt. This could have restored value to Third World debt portfolios while inducing better policies in debtor countries.

v) Finally, it is uncertain whether the resources set aside under the Brady Plan can tackle Mexico's debt swaps, especially if all creditor banks opt for newly issued securities instead of contributing new money.

For the moment, a door has opened to a more realistic approach to the Third World debt problem. Perhaps it was the political stampede to help Mexico that caused a more comprehensive approach to be neglected. As a consequence Mexico, not a likely candidate for success under the Brady Plan, could jeopardize the use of this new approach for other heavily indebted countries. Our comparison of policies and developments in Chile and Mexico indicates that the Brady Plan would be much more likely to succeed in Chile than in Mexico. It could also have served as a signal to other debtors of the rewards of good policy. In any case, the new road to resolving the debt trap is definitely debt reduction that benefits both debtors and creditors. At the same time, the success of the Brady Plan would be assisted by a depoliticising of the debt situation.

NOTES

1. IMF, *World Economic Outlook,* April 1989.
2. World Bank, *World Development Report,* 1988.
3. Krugman, Paul R., "Market-Based Approaches to Debt Reduction", Conference Paper, American Enterprise Institute for Public Policy, April 18, 1989.
4. Krugman, Paul R., "Financing vs. Forgiving a Debt Overhang", Mexico City, March 17-19, 1988.

BIBLIOGRAPHY

AMERICAN EXPRESS' PROPOSAL *International Country Risk Guide,* October 1983.

ANGELOPOULOS, Angelos *A Global Plan for Employment: A New Marshall Plan,* Praeger, New York, 1984.

__________, "A Proposal for Resolving the Global Debt Crisis", *New York Times,* 4th April 1984.

ASKARI, H. and A. PAPALEXOPOULOU *Third World Debt: The Contributions of Financial Innovation to the Financing of Development,* OECD Development Centre Working Paper, February 1989.

AVELLANO, J. and J. RAMOS "Capital Flight in Chile", CIEPLAN, Mimeo, January 1987.

BAILEY, Norman "A Safety Net for Foreign Lending", *Business Week,* 10th January 1983.

BAILEY, Norman, R. LURT and R. ROBINSON "Exchange Participation Notes: An Approach to the International Financial Crisis", CSIS Significant Issues Series, Vol. V, No. 1, Spring 1983, pp. 27-36.

BAKER, James III, the Secretary of the Treasury Statement Before the Joint Annual Meeting of the IMF and the World Bank, 8th October 1985, Seoul, Korea.

BANCO CENTRAL DE CHILE *Provision of the Conversion of External Debt,* Santiago, 1988.

BANK FOR INTERNATIONAL SETTLEMENTS *Annual Report,* June 1987.

BANK FOR INTERNATIONAL SETTLEMENTS "Consultative Paper: Proposals for International Convergence of Capital Measurement and Capital Standards", Committee on Banking Regulations and Supervisory Practices, BIS, December 1987.

BANK FOR INTERNATIONAL SETTLEMENTS *Innovations in International Banking,* April 1986.

BELL, Geoffrey, President of Geoffrey Bell and Co. and Executive Vice President and Director, Schroeder International "Debt Rescheduling – Can the Banking System Cope?", *The Banker,* February 1982, pp. 17-24.

BELL, Geoffrey Speech at March 8, 1983 Financial Times Conference, reported in "Central Banks Urged to Bank International Lending", by Peter Montagnon, *Financial Times,* 9th March 1983, p. 26.

BERGSMAN, Joel and Wayne EDISIS "Debt-Equity Swaps and Foreign Direct Investment in Latin America", IFC Discussion Paper No. 2, 1988.

BHAGWATI, Yagdish *Protectionism,* M.I.T. Press, 1988.

BOLIN, William and Jorge DELCANTO "LDC Debt: Beyond Crisis Management", *Foreign Affairs,* Summer 1983, pp. 1099-1112.

BOLIN, William, Vice Chairman, Bank of America *The Economist Financial Report,* 15th September 1983.

BRADLEY, William, Senator, New Jersey Testimony before the Senate Foreign Relations Committee, Subcommittee on International Economic Policy, United States Congress, 1st February 1983. Reported in *The New York Times,* 2nd February 1983.

BRUNNER, Karl, Professor of Economics at the Universities of Rochester, New York and Berne, Switzerland *Journal of Economic Affairs,* March/April 1983.

BUFFIE, Edward F. *Economic Policy and Foreign Debt in Mexico,* forthcoming in Developing Country Debt and Economic Performance, Vol. 2: country studies, edited by J. Sachs, University of Chicago Press.

CLARK, George J. "Foreign Banks in the Domestic Markets of Developing Countries", in Feinberg and Kallab, eds., *Uncertain Future: Commercial Banks and the Third World,* Rutgers, NJ: Overseas Development Council/Transaction Books, 1984, pp. 79-86.

COMMONWEALTH SECRETARIAT *The Debt Crisis and the World Economy,* Marlborough House, London, 1984.

CORBO, Vittorio "Reforms and Macroeconomic Adjustments in Chile during 1974-84", *World Development,* Vol. 13, No. 8, 1985.

CORBO, Vittorio and Jaime DE MELO "Lessons From the Southern Cone Policy Reforms", World Bank *Research Observer* 2, No. 2, July 1987.

CUMBY, Robert E. and Richard M. LEVICH *On the Definition and Magnitude of Recent Capital Flight,* NBER, 1987.

DALE, Richard S., Guest Scholar at the Brookings Institute "Country Risk and Bank Regulation", *The Banker,* Vol. 133, No. 695, March 1983, pp. 41-48.

DALE, Richard S. "A Proposal for the LDC Debt Problem", *Columbia Journal of World Business,* August 1983, pp. 36-42.

DAVIDSON, Ian and Philip STEPHENS "Mitterand Offers to Waive a Third of Third World Debt", *The Financial Times,* New York, 9th June 1988.

DECARMOY, Herve, Director and Chief Executive International of Midland Bank *A Proposal for Dealing with the Debt Problem,* New York, Trilateral Commission Task Force on Restoring Growth in the Debt-Laden Third World, 1987.

DEVLIN, Robert "The Burden of Debt and the Crisis: Is it Time for a Unilateral Solution", United Nations Economic Commission for Latin America (CEPAL) *Review,* No. 22, April 1984, pp. 107-120.

DORNBUSCH, R. "Our LDC Debt", NBER Working Paper, January 1987.

THE ECONOMIST *Guide to Debt Equity Swaps,* September 1987.

THE ECONOMIST *The Economist's Plan,* 2nd April 1983.

EDWARDS, Sebastian "Stabilization with Liberalization: An Evolution of Ten Years of Chile's Experienced with Free-Market Policies, 1973-1983", *Economic Development and Cultural Change,* p. 33 (January 1985).

EDWARDS, Sebastian and Alejandro Cox Edwards, *Monetarism and Liberalization: The Chilean Experience,* Ballinger Publishing Company, Cambridge, 1988.

FISCHER, Stanley "Economic Growth and Economic Policy", *Symposium on Growth-Oriented Adjustment,* World Bank and the International Monetary Fund, Washington, D.C., 25-27th February 1987.

FRENCH-DAVIS, R. and J. DE GREGORIO "La Renegociacion de la Deuda Externa de Chile en 1985. Antecedentes y Comentarios", *Coleccion Estudios CIEPLAN,* September 1985.

GARCES, Francisco "Comments on Foreign Debt Management in Chile: A Comparative Analysis", paper presented at the *Euromarket* Investment Seminar, Santiago, April 26-28, 1988.

GUTTENTAG, Jack and Richard HERRING "Overexposure of International Banks to Country Risk: Diagnosis and Remedies", Testimony before House Committee on Banking Finance and Urban Affairs, United States Congress, 26th April 1983.

"The Current Crisis in International Banking", Brookings Discussion Papers in International Economics, No. 8, December 1983.

HALLIWELL, Steven E. "Could Debt-Equity Swaps Make Global Debt Manageable", ABA *Banking Journal,* April 1984, p. 74.

HARBERGER, Arnold "Economic Policy and Economic Growth", *World Economic Growth,* ed. by A.C. Harberger Institute for Contemporary Studies, San Francisco, 1984.

HERRHAUSEN, Dr. Alfred, (Deutsche Bank) "Some Ideas on How to Solve the Debt Crisis", Speech to Chase Manhattan Bank, 17th February 1988.

HOFFMEYER, Erik Address at Financial Times' Tenth World Banking Conference, 6th December 1984.

THE HUDSON INSTITUTE *The Economist Financial Report,* 15th September 1983 and *International Country Risk Guide,* October 1983.

INTERNATIONAL MONETARY FUND (IMF) *Annual Report,* 1981-1986.
"Buy-back and the Market Valuation of External Debt", Working Paper, September 1987.
IMF Survey, 16th May 1988.
World Economic Outlook, April 1988.
Prescriptions, *Annual Report 1983,* and address of J. de Larosiere to the 1983 IMF/World Bank Annual Meeting, *IMF Survey,* October 1983, pp. 306-311.

JOHNSON, G.G. and Richard ABRAMs "Aspects of the International Banking Safety Net", IMF Occasional Paper No. 17, Washington, International Monetary Fund, March 1983.

JORGENSON, E. and J. SACHS "Default and Renegotiation of Latin American Bonds in the Interwar Period", Mimeo, Harvard University, May 1988.

KEMP, J. "The Solution to World Debt is World Growth", *The Wall Street Journal,* 10th February 1983.

KENEN, Peter, Economist, Princeton University *The Wall Street Journal,* 8th February 1983 and *International Country Risk Guide,* October 1983.

KRUEGER, Anne D. "Resolving the Debt Crisis and Restoring Developing Countries Creditworthiness", IMF Seminar, 2nd June 1988.

KRUGMAN, P.R. *Financing Vs. Forgiving A Debt Overhang,* Mexico City, March 17-19, 1988.

KRUGMAN, Paul R. "Market-Based Approaches to Debt Reduction", Conference Paper, American Enterprise Institute for Public Policy, April 18, 1989.

KUCZYNSKI, Pedro-Pablo, First Boston Corporation "Latin American Debt: Act Two", *Foreign Affairs,* Vol. 61, No. 2, Winter 1982/1983, pp. 344-364.

LAFALCE, John, Congressman, N.Y. Testimony before House Committee on Banking, Finance and Urban Affairs, United States Congress, 5th March 1987, Congressional Record, p. H-1076.

LANGONI, Carlos G. "The Way Out of the Debt Crisis", *Euromoney,* October 1983, pp. 20-26.

LARRAIN, Felipe *Debt Reduction and the Management of Chilean Debt,* unpublished manuscript, July 1988 (b).
"Public Sector Behavior in a Highly Indebted Country: The Contracting Chilean Experience", The World Bank, January 1988 (a).

LESLIE, Peter "Techniques of Rescheduling: The Latest Lessons", *The Banker,* April 1983, pp. 23-30.

LESSARD, Donald R. and John WILLIAMSON (editors) *Capital Flight and Third World Debt,* Institute for International Economics, Washington, D.C., 1987.

LEVER, Harold "The International Debt Threat: A Concerted Way Out", *The Economist,* 9th July 1983.

LINDBECK, Assar Address before the Royal Institute of International Affairs, 24th January 1984.

MACKWORTH-YOUNG, G.W. "International Banking Crisis", Speech for the British Institute of Management, 17th May 1983.

MAGNIFICO, Giovanni, Central Manager for Operations, Bank of Italy *Journal of Commerce*, 13th December 1982.

MAYER, Martin "Accounting for Troubled Debts", *Wall Street Journal*, 23rd February 1983.

MAYER, Martin "Let the Banks Also Carry the Latin Milestone", *New York Times*, 12th June 1984.

MEISSNER, Charles "Debt: Reform without Governments", Foreign Policy, No. 56, Fall 1984, pp. 81-93.

MELTZER, Alan, Professor of Political Economy and Public Policy, Carnegi-Mellon University "How to Defuse the Debt Bomb", Fortune, 28th November 1983, pp. 137-142.

MELTZER, Alan "There is a Way to Defuse the Debt Bomb", *Financial Times*, 14th December 1983, p. 19.

MENDELSOHN, M.S. *Commercial Banks and the Restructuring of Cross Border Debt*, New York, (Group of Thirty), 1983.

MENDELSOHN, M.S. "The International Debt Crisis", The Banker, Vol. 133, No. 689, July 1983, pp. 33-38.

MORGAN GUARANTY TRUST COMPANY "Global Debt Assessment and Strategy", *World Financial Markets*, June 1983 and October/November 1984.

OAPASSENDA Ministerio, *Macroeconomic Control Plan*, October 1987.

OECD *External Debt of Developing Countries*, Paris, 1984.

____________, *Financing and External Debt of Developing Countries*, Paris, 1988.

PEAT, Marwick, MITCHELL & Co. *Bank Tax Conference*, 1988.
Allowances for Sovereign Risk – An International Survey – Second Edition, Frankfurt, Germany, June 1986.

PRUDENTIAL-BACHE SECURITIES "Banking Industry Outlook", 11th February 1988.

QUITO DECLARATION, February 1983.

REISEN, Helmut *Public Development Country Debt, External Competitiveness, and Required Fiscal Discipline*, Princeton Studies in International Finance, No. 161, September 1989.

REISEN, H. and A. VAN TROTSENBURG *Developing Country Debt: The Budgetary and Transfer Problem*, OECD Development Centre Studies, 1988.

ROBINSON, James II CEO American Express, *A Comprehensive Agenda for LDC Debt and World Trade Breath*, 29th February 1988.

ROHATYN, Felix, Chairman, New York's Municipal Assistance Corporation and Partner, Lazard Freres "A Plan for Stretching Out Global Debt", *Business Week*, 28th February 1983.

ROHATYN, Felix Testimony before the US Congress, Senate Committee on Foreign Relations, 98th Congress 1st Session, Washington, D.C., 17th January 1983.

SACHS, Jeffrey *LDC Debt in the 1980s: Risk and Reforms*, NBER Working Paper No. 861, February 1982.
"Comprehensive Debt Retirement: The Bolivian Example", *Brookings Paper on Economic Activity*, 1987:2.
"Efficient Debt Reduction", Presented at the World Bank Symposium of Dealing with the Debt Crisis, Washington, D.C., January 26-27, 1989.
"The Debt Overhang of Developing Countries", Mimeo, forthcoming in *Debt, Growth and Stabilization: Essays in the Memory of Carlos Diaz Alexandro*, Oxford, Basil Blackwell, 1986.

de SAINT PHELLE, Thibaut (editor) *The International Financial Crisis: An Opportunity for Constructive Action,* Center for Strategic and International Studies of Georgetown University, Washington, D.C., 1983.

SANGINES, Allen *Managing Mexico's External Debt: The Contribution of Debt Reduction Schemes,* Internal Discussion paper, World Bank, January 1989.

SENGUPTA, Arjun, Indian Executive Director IMF In Informal Discussions at IMF.

SHAFIQUL, Islam "Breaking the International Debt Deadlock", Council on Foreign Relations, 1988:2.

SMITH, Fred L. "How the IMF Could Become a Real S&P for International Debt", The Wall Street Journal, 26th July 1983.

SOLOMON, Anthony, President, Federal Reserve Bank of New York *FRBNY Quarterly Review,* Autumn 1983, pp. 1-5.

SOROS, George "The International Debt Problem Revisited", Morgan Stanley Investment Research Paper, March 1984.

SOROS, George "The International Debt Problem – A Prescription", Morgan Stanley Investment Research Papers, May and August 1984.

TELLJOHANN, Kenneth, Corporate Bond Dept., Salomon Brothers Inc., and Richard BUCKHOLZ, PhD, Bond Portfolio Analysis, Salomon Brothers Inc. *The Mexican Bond Exchange Offer: An Analytical Framework,* Salomon Brothers Inc., January 1988.
The Economist, *Financial Report,* 15th September 1983.

UTTING, R.A. In Communication with Mr. deLattre.

WHITEHEAD, John C., Deputy Secretary of State Address before Council on Foreign Relations, New York City, October 21, 1987.

WORLD BANK *World Debt Tables,* 1987-88.
__________, *World Development Report.*

WORLD BANK, IMF, BIS, OECD *External Debt. Definition, Statistical Coverage and Methodology,* Paris 1988.

YASSUKOVICH, Stamislas European Banking Company, *International Country Risk Guide,* October 1983.

ZEDILLO (1985), SOLIS and ZEDILLO (1985), KRAFT (1984), BAILEY and COHEN (1987), BUFFIE (1988), DORNBUSCH (1988).

ZOMBANAKIS, Minos "The International Debt Threat: Way to Avoid a Crash", *The Economist,* 30th April 1983, pp. 11-14.

ZOMBANAKIS, Minos *International Country Risk Guide,* October 1983.

WHERE TO OBTAIN OECD PUBLICATIONS – OÙ OBTENIR LES PUBLICATIONS DE L'OCDE

Argentina – Argentine
CARLOS HIRSCH S.R.L.
Galería Güemes, Florida 165, 4° Piso
1333 Buenos Aires Tel. 30.7122, 331.1787 y 331.2391
Telegram: Hirsch-Baires
Telex: 21112 UAPE-AR. Ref. s/2901
Telefax:(1)331-1787

Australia – Australie
D.A. Book (Aust.) Pty. Ltd.
648 Whitehorse Road, P.O.B 163
Mitcham, Victoria 3132 Tel. (03)873.4411
Telefax: (03)873.5679

Austria – Autriche
OECD Publications and Information Centre
Schedestrasse 7
D-W 5300 Bonn 1 (Germany) Tel. (49.228)21.60.45
Telefax: (49.228)26.11.04

Gerold & Co.
Graben 31
Wien I Tel. (0222)533.50.14

Belgium – Belgique
Jean De Lannoy
Avenue du Roi 202
B-1060 Bruxelles Tel. (02)538.51.69/538.08.41
Telex: 63220 Telefax: (02) 538.08.41

Canada
Renouf Publishing Company Ltd.
1294 Algoma Road
Ottawa, ON K1B 3W8 Tel. (613)741.4333
Telex: 053-4783 Telefax: (613)741.5439
Stores:
61 Sparks Street
Ottawa, ON K1P 5R1 Tel. (613)238.8985
211 Yonge Street
Toronto, ON M5B 1M4 Tel. (416)363.3171

Federal Publications
165 University Avenue
Toronto, ON M5H 3B8 Tel. (416)581.1552
Telefax: (416)581.1743
Les Publications Fédérales
1185 rue de l'Université
Montréal, PQ H3B 3A7 Tel.(514)954-1633

Les Éditions La Liberté Inc.
3020 Chemin Sainte-Foy
Sainte-Foy, PQ G1X 3V6 Tel. (418)658.3763
Telefax: (418)658.3763

Denmark – Danemark
Munksgaard Export and Subscription Service
35, Nørre Søgade, P.O. Box 2148
DK-1016 København K Tel. (45 33)12.85.70
Telex: 19431 MUNKS DK Telefax: (45 33)12.93.87

Finland – Finlande
Akateeminen Kirjakauppa
Keskuskatu 1, P.O. Box 128
00100 Helsinki Tel. (358 0)12141
Telex: 125080 Telefax: (358 0)121.4441

France
OECD/OCDE
Mail Orders/Commandes par correspondance:
2, rue André-Pascal
75775 Paris Cédex 16 Tel. (33-1)45.24.82.00
Bookshop/Librairie:
33, rue Octave-Feuillet
75016 Paris Tel. (33-1)45.24.81.67
(33-1)45.24.81.81
Telex: 620 160 OCDE
Telefax: (33-1)45.24.85.00 (33-1)45.24.81.76

Librairie de l'Université
12a, rue Nazareth
13100 Aix-en-Provence Tel. 42.26.18.08
Telefax : 42.26.63.26

Germany – Allemagne
OECD Publications and Information Centre
Schedestrasse 7
D-W 5300 Bonn 1 Tel. (0228)21.60.45
Telefax: (0228)26.11.04

Greece – Grèce
Librairie Kauffmann
28 rue du Stade
105 64 Athens Tel. 322.21.60
Telex: 218187 LIKA Gr

Hong Kong
Swindon Book Co. Ltd.
13 - 15 Lock Road
Kowloon, Hong Kong Tel. 366.80.31
Telex: 50 441 SWIN HX Telefax: 739.49.75

Iceland – Islande
Mál Mog Menning
Laugavegi 18, Pósthólf 392
121 Reykjavik Tel. 15199/24240

India – Inde
Oxford Book and Stationery Co.
Scindia House
New Delhi 110001 Tel. 331.5896/5308
Telex: 31 61990 AM IN
Telefax: (11)332.5993
17 Park Street
Calcutta 700016 Tel. 240832

Indonesia – Indonésie
Pdii-Lipi
P.O. Box 269/JKSMG/88
Jakarta 12790 Tel. 583467
Telex: 62 875

Ireland – Irlande
TDC Publishers – Library Suppliers
12 North Frederick Street
Dublin 1 Tel. 744835/749677
Telex: 33530 TDCP EI Telefax: 748416

Italy – Italie
Libreria Commissionaria Sansoni
Via Benedetto Fortini, 120/10
Casella Post. 552
50125 Firenze Tel. (055)64.54.15
Telex: 570466 Telefax: (055)64.12.57
Via Bartolini 29
20155 Milano Tel. 36.50.83
La diffusione delle pubblicazioni OCSE viene assicurata dalle principali librerie ed anche da:

Editrice e Libreria Herder
Piazza Montecitorio 120
00186 Roma Tel. 679.46.28
Telex: NATEL I 621427

Libreria Hoepli
Via Hoepli 5
20121 Milano Tel. 86.54.46
Telex: 31.33.95 Telefax: (02)805.28.86

Libreria Scientifica
Dott. Lucio de Biasio 'Aeiou'
Via Meravigli 16
20123 Milano Tel. 805.68.98
Telefax: 800175

Japan – Japon
OECD Publications and Information Centre
Landic Akasaka Building
2-3-4 Akasaka, Minato-ku
Tokyo 107 Tel. (81.3)3586.2016
Telefax: (81.3)3584.7929

Korea – Corée
Kyobo Book Centre Co. Ltd.
P.O. Box 1658, Kwang Hwa Moon
Seoul Tel. (REP)730.78.91
Telefax: 735.0030

Malaysia/Singapore – Malaisie/Singapour
Co-operative Bookshop Ltd.
University of Malaya
P.O. Box 1127, Jalan Pantai Baru
59700 Kuala Lumpur
Malaysia Tel. 756.5000/756.5425
Telefax: 757.3661

Information Publications Pte. Ltd.
Pei-Fu Industrial Building
24 New Industrial Road No. 02-06
Singapore 1953 Tel. 283.1786/283.1798
Telefax: 284.8875

Netherlands – Pays-Bas
SDU Uitgeverij
Christoffel Plantijnstraat 2
Postbus 20014
2500 EA's-Gravenhage Tel. (070 3)78.99.11
Voor bestellingen: Tel. (070 3)78.98.80
Telex: 32486 stdru Telefax: (070 3)47.63.51

New Zealand – Nouvelle-Zélande
GP Publications Ltd.
Customer Services
33 The Esplanade - P.O. Box 38-900
Petone, Wellington
Tel. (04)685-555 Telefax: (04)685-333

Norway – Norvège
Narvesen Info Center - NIC
Bertrand Narvesens vei 2
P.O. Box 6125 Etterstad
0602 Oslo 6 Tel. (02)57.33.00
Telex: 79668 NIC N Telefax: (02)68.19.01

Pakistan
Mirza Book Agency
65 Shahrah Quaid-E-Azam
Lahore 3 Tel. 66839
Telex: 44886 UBL PK. Attn: MIRZA BK

Portugal
Livraria Portugal
Rua do Carmo 70-74
Apart. 2681
1117 Lisboa Codex Tel.: 347.49.82/3/4/5
Telefax: (01) 347.02.64

Singapore/Malaysia – Singapour/Malaisie
See "Malaysia/Singapore" – Voir «Malaisie/Singapour»

Spain – Espagne
Mundi-Prensa Libros S.A.
Castelló 37, Apartado 1223
Madrid 28001 Tel. (91) 431.33.99
Telex: 49370 MPLI Telefax: 575.39.98

Libreria Internacional AEDOS
Consejo de Ciento 391
08009-Barcelona Tel. (93) 301.86.15
Telefax: (93) 317.01.41

Sri Lanka
Centre for Policy Research
c/o Mercantile Credit Ltd.
55, Janadhipathi Mawatha
Colombo 1 Tel. 438471-9, 440346
Telex: 21138 VAVALEX CE Telefax: 94.1.448900

Sweden – Suède
Fritzes Fackboksföretaget
Box 16356
Regeringsgatan 12
103 27 Stockholm Tel. (08)23.89.00
Telex: 12387 Telefax: (08)20.50.21

Subscription Agency/Abonnements:
Wennergren-Williams AB
Nordenflychtsvägen 74
Box 30004
104 25 Stockholm Tel. (08)13.67.00
Telex: 19937 Telefax: (08)618.62.32

Switzerland – Suisse
OECD Publications and Information Centre
Schedestrasse 7
D-W 5300 Bonn 1 (Germany) Tel. (49.228)21.60.45
Telefax: (49.228)26.11.04

Librairie Payot
6 rue Grenus
1211 Genève 11 Tel. (022)731.89.50
Telex: 28356
Subscription Agency – Service des Abonnements
Naville S.A.
7, rue Lévrier
1201 Genève Tél.: (022) 732.24.00
Telefax: (022) 738.48.03

Maditec S.A.
Chemin des Palettes 4
1020 Renens/Lausanne Tel. (021)635.08.65
Telefax: (021)635.07.80

United Nations Bookshop/Librairie des Nations-Unies
Palais des Nations
1211 Genève 10 Tel. (022)734.60.11 (ext. 48.72)
Telex: 289696 (Attn: Sales) Telefax: (022)733.98.79

Taiwan – Formose
Good Faith Worldwide Int'l. Co. Ltd.
9th Floor, No. 118, Sec. 2
Chung Hsiao E. Road
Taipei Tel. 391.7396/391.7397
Telefax: (02) 394.9176

Thailand – Thaïlande
Suksit Siam Co. Ltd.
1715 Rama IV Road, Samyan
Bangkok 5 Tel. 251.1630

Turkey – Turquie
Kültur Yayinlari Is-Türk Ltd. Sti.
Atatürk Bulvari No. 191/Kat. 21
Kavaklidere/Ankara Tel. 25.07.60
Dolmabahce Cad. No. 29
Besiktas/Istanbul Tel. 160.71.88
Telex: 43482B

United Kingdom – Royaume-Uni
HMSO
Gen. enquiries Tel. (071) 873 0011
Postal orders only:
P.O. Box 276, London SW8 5DT
Personal Callers HMSO Bookshop
49 High Holborn, London WC1V 6HB
Telex: 297138 Telefax: 071 873 2000
Branches at: Belfast, Birmingham, Bristol, Edinburgh, Manchester

United States – États-Unis
OECD Publications and Information Centre
2001 L Street N.W., Suite 700
Washington, D.C. 20036-4910 Tel. (202)785.6323
Telefax: (202)785.0350

Venezuela
Libreria del Este
Avda F. Miranda 52, Aptdo. 60337
Edificio Galipán
Caracas 106 Tel. 951.1705/951.2307/951.1297
Telegram: Libreste Caracas

Yugoslavia – Yougoslavie
Jugoslovenska Knjiga
Knez Mihajlova 2, P.O. Box 36
Beograd Tel.: (011)621.992
Telex: 12466 jk bgd Telefax: (011)625.970

Orders and inquiries from countries where Distributors have not yet been appointed should be sent to: OECD Publications Service, 2 rue André-Pascal, 75775 Paris Cedex 16, France.

Les commandes provenant de pays où l'OCDE n'a pas encore désigné de distributeur devraient être adressées à : OCDE, Service des Publications, 2, rue André-Pascal, 75775 Paris Cédex 16, France.

75669–4/91

OECD PUBLICATIONS, 2 rue André-Pascal, 75775 PARIS CEDEX 16
PRINTED IN FRANCE
(41 91 07 1) ISBN 92-64-13496-4 - No. 45539 1991